Galloping Along the Old West Trails

Galloping Along the Old West Trails

An Integrated Social Studies Unit

Gary M. Garfield
Suzanne McDonough

Illustrations by Sheryl Tongue
Carmen Lindsay

1997
TEACHER IDEAS PRESS
A Division of
Libraries Unlimited, Inc.
Englewood, Colorado

TEACHER IDEAS PRESS
A Division of
LIBRARIES UNLIMITED, INC.
P.O. Box 6633
Englewood, CO 80155-6633
1-800-237-6124

Constance Hardesty, *Project Editor*

Jane Olivier, *Production*

Sheryl Tongue, *Design and Composition*

Library of Congress Cataloging-in-Publication Data

Garfield, Gary M.
    Galloping along the old west trails : an integrated social studies unit / Gary M. Garfield and Suzanne McDonough : illustrated by Sheryl Tongue and Carmen Lindsay.
    xxii, 183 p. 22×28 cm.
    Includes bibliographical references.
    ISBN 1-56308-475-9 (pbk.)
    1. West (U.S.)--History--Study and teaching--Activity programs.
2. West (U.S.)--Description and travel--Study and teaching--Activity programs. 3. Frontier and pioneer life--West (U.S.)--Study and teaching--Activity programs. 4. United States--Territorial expansion--Study and teaching--Activity programs. I. McDonough, Suzanne, 1959–   . II. Title.
F591.G227 1996
372.89´044--dc20   96-9879
                                              CIP

Contents

Introduction

Howdy partners, buckaroos, ropers, cowgirls, cowboys, and anyone else hiding out in this here prairie schooner waiting to begin the trip overland to the Pacific Coast. Come join us—two teachers who rustled up some old boots, western duds, dull spurs, a kerchief (got to have a big kerchief), hats, characters from the Old West, elementary school children, and, of course, a fine horse—on a journey you'll never forget.

This is not our first journey. We've hit the trail before after only a few days of planning. We shared this magnificent trek with our friends, the Cowboy and his good ole horse, Kaper King. For six weeks we gathered 'round the computer, wrote letters, and tracked the journey as a caring family of western adventurers and learners. This book makes it possible for you to saddle up and take your class galloping along the Old West trails.

OVERVIEW

Westward expansion has always been a great teaching and learning vehicle—that is, if you hide the history book under a bale of hay and feed the test questions to the coyotes. As our class gathered around the campfire (that is, the computer), we experienced a new way to learn, a new way to seek information, and a new way to teach.

With a classroom teacher, a university professor, and a classroom of children who expected something new on the horizon, we were on our way.

How We Started

It was over a cup of coffee that our Cowboy and the journey west were born. We thought about all the traditional, and not-so-traditional, ways that children are introduced to the 1850s. We talked about the books, the videos, the museums, and the field trips. We discussed engagement, learning through doing, and authentic assessment. We knew what we had to do: We were *all*—teachers and students—going to travel west together, without ever leaving the classroom. We knew we could create a western character—the Cowboy—that would bond with the children through letters he would send them. We would speak to the children through the Cowboy's letters, and the children would develop a meaningful relationship with the Cowboy. We hoped the activity would also create a new relationship with learning, history, social science, and, of course, the westward expansion.

Although we used telecommunications to send letters to the children, you could just as effectively photocopy the letters in this book and mail them or deliver them personally.

How It Worked

The Cowboy sent a letter to the children every day for six weeks. In the letters he described the places, feelings, and characters he encountered as he moved across the territories. Most of the letters also introduced a generic period character. Each of these characters wrote a letter describing life in the West (and, sometimes, questions, issues, or problems for discussion or reflection) to the children to enhance their understanding of the people who settled the West.

Meanwhile, back in the classroom, the messages skipped across the computer screen before they were printed and posted for all to see. (This reflects how news was delivered and then posted, after the recipient read it, outside the newspaper office in Old West towns.) The teacher provided enrichment or extension activities to complement each letter.

Oral and silent reading, hands-on engagement, and cooperative learning addressed all the modalities. The children experienced the geography, the characters, the inventions, the joys, and the hardships of life in the Old West.

The children plotted the progress of the Cowboy as he moved west from St. Louis, south on the Shawnee Trail, north on the Chisholm Trail, and west on the Oregon Trail. After many weeks featuring cattle drives, storms, prairie fires, encounters with explorers and Native Americans, river crossings, visits with recent settlers, and other adventures, the Cowboy and all the other characters he encountered found their way to the classroom. They walked right up the front walkway onto the school grounds and shared food, song, stories, and of course, the fine ole horse.

How to Use This Book

This book includes letters from the Cowboy and other characters he meets during his journey west. The letters are sent to the children almost daily as they study westward expansion. Though the Cowboy is the main character, the cast is large, with all of the characters you would expect to find in the Old West—banker, shopkeeper, and so forth. The Cowboy writes regularly, but the other characters write only once.

Following each letter are one or more activities the students can do to further their understanding of the topics discussed in the letter. For example, following a letter about weather are activities related to weather.

The Online Stagecoach

Two disks (Windows and Macintosh compatible) attached to the back cover contain the letters in their entirety. This allows you to give a disk to a volunteer to use to send the letters to you via telecommunications. The volunteer simply sends the letters straight from the disk in one computer to your computer. This is a simple beginners' project, good for teachers and students (and volunteers) new to telecommunications.

If you have several volunteers taking on the roles of the various characters, you will need to circulate or copy the disk so that each volunteer can send his or her letter to your class at the appropriate time. Or, you can copy each character's letter from the master disk onto individual disks for each volunteer to use.

Doin' It the Old-Fashioned Way

Even teachers without telecommunications capabilities can do this project with their students. The letters can be sent to the students by the U.S. Postal Service, secret deliveries (slipped under the door), or by Pony Express. Your imagination is the limit. The important thing is that the letters come regularly. The letters can be read aloud or silently, alone or in a group.

Extensions and Enrichment

No matter what mode of delivery you choose, twentieth-century folks soon will be transformed into mavericks of the Old West.

The scores of extension activities linked to the letters focus on journals, diaries, reading and literature; map reading; art and music; science; computer technology and telecommunications; and activities, like cleaning horseshoes, that don't fall into any curricular category.

Listen for the click, ring, and squeal of your modem (or create another signal, like jingling spurs, to start each session). Your students will ask, "Is that the Cowboy?" Gather 'round the computer (or that Old West newspaper office) as we tell stories about our journey west.

WHAT YOU NEED TO GALLOP ALONG

Setting out on this journey is like making a big kettle of Mountain Stew. You start with a few essential ingredients, add some others that are not so essential, throw in a little salt, then stir and simmer it until it is hearty and rich.

The Cast of Characters

The main character of this project is the Cowboy. He will send letters regularly. However, there is a large supporting cast of characters the Cowboy meets along the way. These characters send only one letter each to your students. You can include as many or as few supporting characters as you wish.

The Cowboy. This book contains a collection of letters from the Cowboy, plus activities to help further students' understanding of the topics addressed in the Cowboy's letters. Feel free to change the letters, add new ones, or create new activities.

You will need to find a dedicated volunteer to take on the role of the Cowboy. This volunteer will send about 30 letters, 1 each day for 6 weeks. Our Cowboy was one of the authors, a university professor. But your Cowboy could be a teacher; the principal; a real, honest-to-goodness, no-shower-in-a-week cowboy; or a parent. (Whoever becomes the cowboy will soon begin to walk differently, carry himself or herself a few inches taller, and talk with a twang. Hoof pick, saddlebags, and beef jerky will take on a whole new meaning.)

All the Cowboy has to do is send the letters via telecommunications, in the mail, in person (slip them under the door), or by Pony Express. How the letters get to you doesn't matter as long as they arrive. If you miss one, don't worry. Tell the kids the Cowboy got held up in a bad snowfall in the Rockies.

The characters. Letters from characters, for example, the banker or shopkeeper, can be sent to the class the same way the Cowboy sends his letters. Here, however, timing is everything. To teach some really special things about the characters, their letters need to arrive at just the right time.

Who sends these letters? A different person can send each one. Whoever sends the letter from a particular character "becomes" that character.

Here are some suggestions:

★ **Students** can send the letters as part of a research project. As they research a particular topic—banking and money in the Old West, for example—they compare the information they are gathering to the information in the banker's letter provided in this book. They can learn enough about the characters to act them out (role play) for other members of the class.

★ **Parents** can take on the roles of the characters, again using the letters provided or adding originals. The time commitment is minimal: They send the letter and show up in costume for the party at the end of the unit. Seek parent volunteers during back-to-school night. Who wants to be the banker? The town undertaker? The stable keeper?

★ **Teachers** can be characters, too. You may find volunteers in your building or in your district, or you may find far-off collaborators online.

★ **Students in teacher education classes** are good candidates for characters, because you can be sure their level of interest (in teaching, not cattle dogging) is high. To tap into this enthusiastic cadre, contact a local (or not-so-local) university's college of education and its elementary social science methods classes. Remember, your characters don't have to be nearby if you are using telecommunications. Wherever there is a computer, telephone line, and modem, you can be there!

★ **Businesses** are untapped resources with great potential. More and more businesses and corporations are trying to forge links with community agencies, and many have employees with telecommunications expertise. If the employees don't have experience, they can still provide enthusiasm. You can all learn together.

★ **Peers** in the upper grades or in middle school or high school can play the supporting characters. This can be especially fun if your student volunteers have already completed the unit. They can return to the classroom as one of the characters they got to know when they were involved in the unit.

The Cybertrail

On the Old West trail, you needed a good horse, a strong pack, saddle, reins, blanket, personal gear, dried meat, and a good hat. On the cybertrail, you'll need a computer, telephone line, modem, and telecommunications software.

Hardware.   Start with a computer that has enough memory to run a variety of programs, including telecommunications, word processing, and graphics.

The computer should also support a few peripherals—the modem, of course, and a printer. (If you're lucky enough to have a multimedia computer, you can even listen to music from the CD drive or from files you download from the Internet. But that's not really necessary to get started.) If you have any questions about what requirements you need for your computer to handle the basic telecommunications functions associated with this project, you can ask your district technology manager (or the school's informal "tech wizard"). But be careful: He or she will want to tell you about all the latest and greatest gear. That's like going on the Old West trail with a brand new sleeping bag. Useful, yes, but the old bedroll works just as well.

You certainly need a modem, which, in effects, translates (modulates) the data you type to sound so that it can be sent over telephone lines (or cable) to another computer. At the destination, the modem translates (demodulates) the sound signal back to data. That's a pretty bare-bones, simplified version of what actually happens, but you don't really need to know the technical details to succeed with your project.

Essential for telecommunications is a dedicated telephone line, which is a line that is separate from the office clusters. Having a dedicated line means you won't get disconnected whenever a call comes into the school. The telephone line will serve you very much like the telegraph served correspondents in the Old West, transmitting messages from Abilene to St. Louis.

A cassette tape deck or CD player is nice if you want to listen to music from the Old West while you work, but it has little bearing on whether the Cowboy reaches his destination.

Software.   Telecommunications software tells your computer and modem what to do in order to send or receive messages. It coordinates, instructs, and "directs traffic" between your computer, the modem, the telephone lines, and the modem and computer at the other end of your connection. All kinds of technical details are involved, but everything you need to know is in the manual that comes with the software.

Telecommunications software comes with most modems. In addition, it is included in recent versions of Windows (look in the Accessories group for Terminal). Most new computers come with a variety of software already installed. You may find a telecommunications program there.

If you don't have telecommunications software, you can purchase easy-to-use software from a discount outlet or catalog. Shareware packagers also offer cut-rate telecommunications programs. Finally, if you have a telecommunications program but you want a different one, you can use your current program to connect to the Internet or an online service (such as America Online, Prodigy, CompuServe, or Microsoft Network), where you can download public domain or shareware programs.

On our Macintosh computers, we have used Microphone, Global Village, and Mac Terminal. Windows Terminal, WinPro, and ProComm are telecommunications programs frequently used on IBMs and compatibles.

Using your modem.   If you are going to send the letters via modem, be sure you have a modem and telecommunications software and know how to use them. Practice corresponding online with a friend a few times to get the hang of telecommunicating. Be sure every person who will be sending messages (including the Cowboy and all of the characters) is comfortable with the process before you start this project.

To Receive
Turn on the computer and "tell" the telecommunications software to prepare to receive calls. The procedure varies slightly with each software program. Usually, you'll double-click on your telecommunications software icon to open the program, then use menus or icons to get to the "receive" mode. Look for topics like "transfers" or "receiving messages" in the manual that came with your telecommunications software.

To Send
Turn on the computer. Open the telecommunications software and prepare to send the letter. Every software program is slightly different: You may use icons and pull-down menus, or you may need to type in commands. Either way, the process is fairly simple. As the message is sent, you may see on the screen an ongoing tally of the number of bytes transferred and the time elapsed. Most software programs give you some kind of signal when the transfer is complete. (Our computers made noise; yours may flash a message on the screen.)

The first time you and your partners exchange messages, it may seem a little awkward. Again, be sure everyone involved in the project is comfortable sending messages before it is their turn to do it. Soon, the procedure will be as easy as swattin' flies off a horse's back. Remember, we shared almost all of the letters in this book with one another in this fashion. If we can do it, you can, too!

If you need a helping hand, consult

✶ the manual that came with the telecommunications software or modem;

✶ on-screen help (look for a help button or menu item at the top of the screen when you have your telecommunications software open);

* your school or district technology mentor;
* experienced teachers (post a note in the teachers' room);
* a computer whiz on staff;
* a knowledgeable student;
* the college of education at a local university;
* members of a local user's group;
* the staff of a local computer store.

Knowledge and Experience

So, what do you, the teacher, need to know to set off on a journey of your own?

First, you need to know the basics of telecommunications. Read your software manual or a beginner's guide to telecommunications—or better yet, get some hands-on training from an experienced person. It takes only a few minutes to master the basics.

Next, you need to be willing to learn as you go. Don't be afraid to ask for assistance. You can even e-mail us, if you get stuck. Our e-mail addresses are

Garfield: gmgarfield@csupomona.edu

McDonough: smdono@cyberg8t.com

You don't need to be a historian of the 1850s or the westward expansion. You might want to review the books listed in the bibliography at the end of this book. Again, you can consult an expert. Remember, if you are online, the expert doesn't need to be local to be accessible. Consult an online resource bulletin board where you may confer with others who have that expertise.

Coordination

Meet with colleagues who are interested in the project. Don't restrict yourself to official meetings, staff development sessions, and minimum days. Meet over dinner, coffee, or dessert; after school; or at private homes.

A Student-Centered Approach

Galloping Along the Old West Trails assumes that the approach to learning centers on the student. With the advent of new delivery systems (like telecommunications) and the willingness of teachers to take on new roles, we must think differently about the way children learn and the way we teach. *Galloping Along the Old West Trails* provides a base from which children can assume leadership, take the initiative, become motivated, and develop concepts and relationships. Our students use modern technology to not just learn about but to experience (in a limited form of virtual reality) the history of the Old West. As teachers, we must *let* this learning happen, not make it happen. We need to think carefully about the seemingly infinite resources available to children in discovery and inquiry. We supply the focus, but our students decide what they will see.

Inquiry and the Researcher

As teachers, we promote the concept of the student as researcher, problem solver, and decision maker. We support this concept as we travel with our characters. We ask students to research the time period, characters, and events. As the western scene becomes clearer, so does the student inquiry.

We ask questions related to the motivation of our cowboy. We also ask questions related to issues of exploration; meeting new friends; being lonely; relationships with people different from us; understanding diversity; and the ethics of economics, power, and progress. Through research, students ask and answer relevant questions. Through this inquiry, whether individual or cooperative, the learners sense a potency in their ability to seek information and come to new understandings.

A Final Word: Be Creative!

If you are excited, all the participants—both students and volunteers—will be excited, too. Be creative, take risks, don't always go by the old book (or this one, either). Although a complete set of materials is included in print and on disk, feel free to be spontaneous and creative. Design your own activities, modify the letters, add new characters, or change the traits of existing ones. Make this your project. Never let our ideas inhibit yours. Let these resources be your guide, with the ultimate goal of climbing in the saddle and taking the reins yourself.

Traveling the Trail

A Record of the Cowboy's Progress Along the Trail

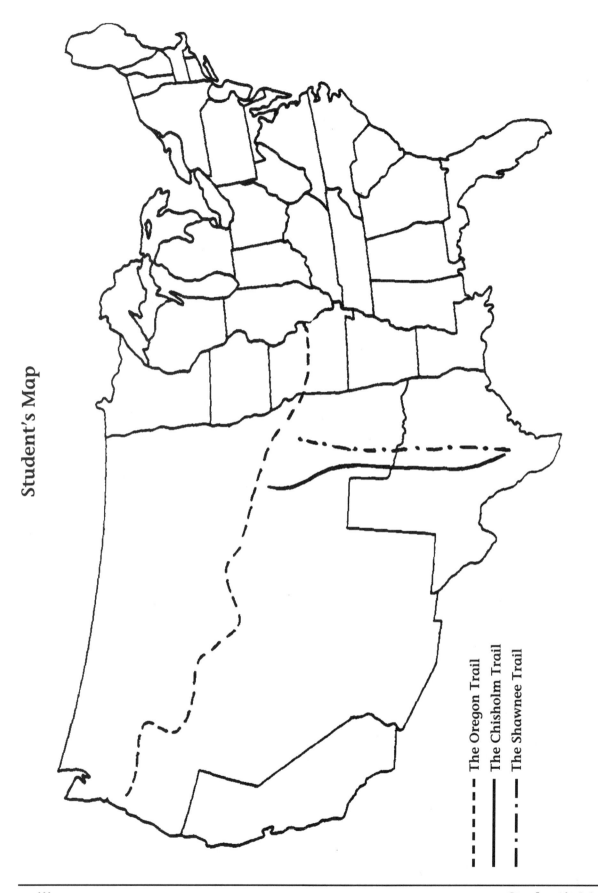

The Oregon Trail
The Chisholm Trail
The Shawnee Trail

Student's Map

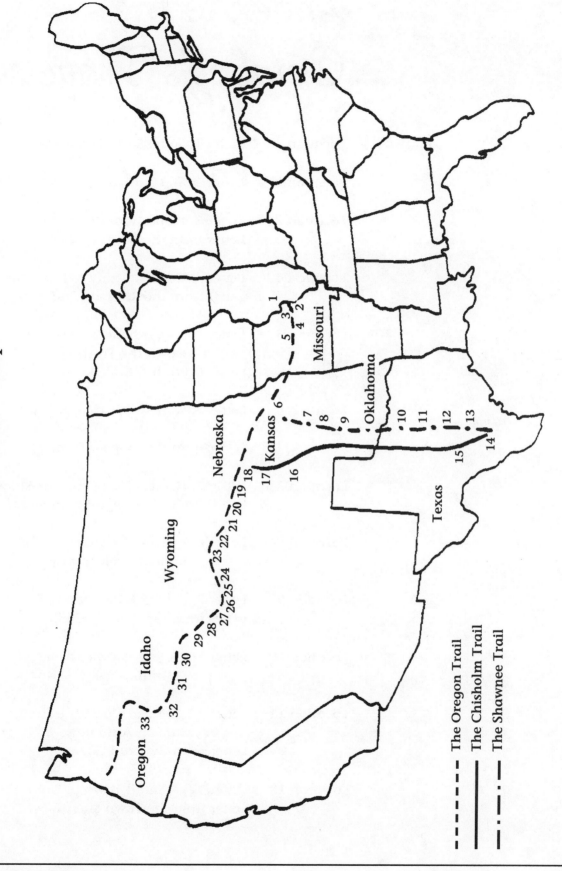

The Oregon Trail
The Chisholm Trail
The Shawnee Trail

Index to the Cowboy's Travels

Letters from the Cowboy

A Record of His Adventures Along the Trail

Letter 1
Some Early Thoughts

I am young and can easily make the trip. The family farm is in good hands with my two brothers and their families, and I am feeling the need to find something of my own. I know that the original gold run is about eight years behind us, but folks are still heading west in droves. You hear about friends selling the farm or moving from town looking for something new. Sometimes, you hear they made it and are doing well, and other times the news of their tragedy is telegraphed home, where everyone shares the sorrow. I suppose that is the risk we take for adventure.

My reason is a quiet one. I can't say I am going west for riches or for reward. Nor is it to get away from what I have. It is truly so beautiful here. The valleys are so green from spring through fall, and the rivers and lakes are so blue and bountiful with wildlife. This must be paradise, yet I feel compelled to move on. I don't understand it, but I know I have to do this. This is the day I will leave, and I am packed up and ready. I will be taking the things I can carry on my horse, Kaper King—some things for trading and others for special remembrance.

When I look at my reflection in the mirror, I wonder what I will look like in a couple of months. I am clean shaven, except for my mustache, and my hair is brown with a hint of premature gray. I put on my old leather vest atop my faded blue work shirt, my well-worked and weather-cracked brown boots, and my firm, black rough-out leather hat. Chaps, long underwear, extra pants, socks, and a fleece-lined coat are already in my saddle packs, which I can easily hoist up onto my

From *Galloping Along the Old West Trails* © 1996   Teacher Ideas Press   1-800-237-6124.

horse's back. I also have a few tools, like a small hatchet and some leather straps for fixing things. Anything else I need I will buy, make, trade, or work for along the way.

Outside, I check Kaper King for soundness. We are alone. I look in Kaper King's kind, dark eyes and say a few words of encouragement to him. I suppose those words are really to calm my anxiety and to convince me I am doing the right thing. I hear the door of the farmhouse swing open. My family stands on the porch. As they walk toward me, I feel their envy and sense their heartache. It may very well be that I never again will see the family that I love. We hug and kiss, and they each say some nice words to me. My sister hands me packets of food to help me on the first leg of my journey to St. Louis.

I put one foot in the stirrup. With a leg over, I am in the saddle, ready to begin my new life. As Kaper King walks slowly away from the farmhouse, I keep looking back to see those I love disappear behind the trees. I know that, although I may not see them again, they will always be in my heart, wherever I go. One final wave, though no one can see me, and all I can hear is the sound of my horse's feet stepping forward.

Sincerely,
The Cowboy

From *Galloping Along the Old West Trails*   © 1996   Teacher Ideas Press   1-800-237-6124.

Activity

I don't get up in the morning and ponder what I'm going to look like today. I know my wide brim hat, my red bandanna, my chaps and jingling spurs, plus a whole lot more will make my job tolerable. Follow me to the bunkhouse, and I'll be happy to show you my gear.

Paper Cowboy

Objective
Students will create a paper cowboy, identify the articles of clothing he wears, and explain the function of each.

Terms

longjohns	This woolen, all-in-one underwear provided warmth.
trousers	Heavy wool or cotton pants withstood the rugged wear and tear of the cowboy's daily activities.
suspenders	Kept the cowboy's pants from falling down. They were much safer than a belt when bulldogging and branding cattle. A belt was more likely to become snagged and cause injury.
hat	Protected the cowboy from the elements. During severe weather, it kept rain and snow out of his face. The broad rim shaded his eyes and neck and protected him from low-hanging branches.
shirt	Long-sleeved wool or cotton shirts protected the cowboy's arms and provided warmth.
bandanna	A big handkerchief that could be used to mask the cowboy's mouth and nose to keep out the dirt and grime that was kicked up on the trail.
chaps	These leather leggings were worn over trousers to prevent the cowboy's clothing from being torn and his legs from being scraped, cut, or bitten.
cowboy boots	Cowboy boots are tall leather boots with pointed toes and high, tapered heels. The design of the boot made it easy to slip the feet into the stirrups. The boot's heel kept the boot from slipping through the stirrup, and the high sides protected the cowboy's legs.
spurs	Fastened to the boots' heels, spurs were used to get the horse's attention when the cowboy pushed his heels against the horse's sides.
lasso	A rope made of leather or hemp used to catch horses and cattle.

From *Galloping Along the Old West Trails* © 1996 Teacher Ideas Press 1-800-237-6124.

Materials

★ Photocopies of the cowboy outline, one for each student
★. Construction paper of various colors or wrapping paper
★ Scissors, tape, glue

Procedure

Distribute one photocopy of the cowboy outline (see page 6) to each student. Students cut out the cowboy and paste the cutout to a piece of tagboard. This provides strength to the cutout. Students color the longjohns on the cutout. (Be sure they are red!)

Students draw and cut out pants, shirt, suspenders, a bandanna, boots and spurs, and a hat, using construction paper or wrapping paper. They tape or glue the clothes onto the cutout.

Encourage students to:

★ add a beard to the cowboy;
★ snip the edge of the chaps to create the fringed look of leather;
★ add geometric lines to the bandanna to make it look like printed fabric; or
★ draw western motifs on the boots to create the look of tooled leather.

Activity

5

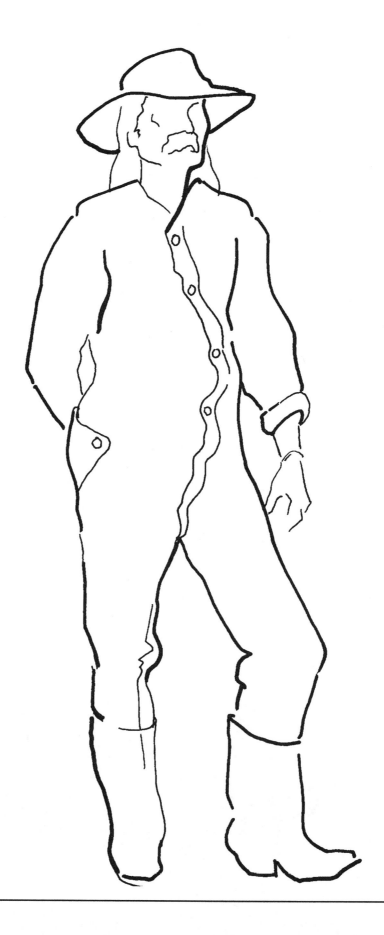

Activity

Letter 2
St. Louis, 1857

This is my first day in St. Louis. They call this big city the Gateway to the West. I've been here a few times before, but I never thought much about what St. Louis means and how this bustling city got its name. It is an amazing place. It is so loud. So very different from the farm. I haven't talked to a lot of folks around here; everyone is so very busy. Wagons everywhere, people on horseback, and excitement in the air. It seems that everyone is going West. I'm just one of many who are preparing for the journey. I hope you can see a picture of the place in your mind.

I arrived here yesterday from our small farm about 100 miles north of here on the Mississippi River, just east of Quincy. Because of bad weather, it took me almost six days to make the journey. It is late in the year to be starting out, but I am hoping I can make it quite a ways west before the snow starts falling. Indian summer will be here soon, and I expect I will see the trees turn to beautiful colors. I know I will miss that when I leave this place behind. There is something about all those oranges and reds turning in the fall that lets a man know he is really alive. I always look forward to seeing those huge mounds of bright leaves piled high by the old barn. To me, it's a sign of a new year. The animals begin to get ready for winter, and people start acting differently. All summer long the stove in the cabin is cold, but in the fall it starts up again, and you can smell the burning wood all across the valley. I remember Ma cooking a hearty bean soup for the evening meal.

St. Louis, 1857

From *Galloping Along the Old West Trails* © 1996 Teacher Ideas Press 1-800-237-6124.

Friends who have already made the journey tell me that far West, there is just one long season. But, I guess it's a new beginning for me, so maybe it's all right that things will be different.

I will start my journey in a day or so. I hope to connect with some other folks so we can travel together. Otherwise, I'll have to make the first leg of my journey with just my horse, Kaper King, for company.

You'd like Kaper. He is a big, light gray horse. From across the hill, he looks almost white. He has a handsome face and kind eyes and is a fine, powerful horse. He is good to me, and I try to be good to him. We are best friends, and we will make this journey together. We are both strong and healthy, so our chances are good. Yet, we still don't really know what we will find out there. I will take some basic supplies, and I hope to hunt, trade, and work along the way. We will do what we have to do.

I'm beginning to wonder if I made the right decision. It is a difficult choice to leave friends and family for the unknown. I'm tired after the trip to St. Louis, and it's getting dark, so I should find a comfortable place to stay for the night. I'll be writing to you soon. Look for my letters.

Sincerely,
The Cowboy

Activity

As the Cowboy travels along the Oregon, Shawnee, and Chisholm trails, it is important for the children to understand and see where his journey takes him. Use a large classroom or hallway map as an impressive visual aid to plot his "progress" for all to see. This activity will expand your curriculum for teaching in the content areas of geography and mapping skills.

Follow Me West

Objective

On a large map, the students will follow the route of the Cowboy as he and Kaper King travel west. Students determine and plot the Cowboy's location based on his letters. In addition, the location of each character encountered will be marked on the map.

Materials

* ⋆ Overhead projector
* ⋆ Black line master of the United States (see page xviii)
* ⋆ Self-adhesive stickers (dots, stars, etc.)
* ⋆ Yarn, markers, crayons, push pins, stapler
* ⋆ Miscellaneous items to represent characters

Procedure

Make a large wall map of the United States using an overhead projector and the provided black line master. (Of course, a floor-to-ceiling map would be best.) You may choose to outline all 48 mainland states or be more authentic to the time period and only outline political boundaries of states and territories of the 1850s.

As you begin receiving letters from the Cowboy, discuss the places he writes about and locate them on the map. Plot and mark your map with self-adhesive stickers that students can use to label the names of cities, rivers, and mountains. Each time the Cowboy meets a new character, label the location where the encounter took place with something that represents the character's occupation. It might be a picture from a book, a postcard, a sample of one of the activities in this book, or a student drawing.

Here are some examples of how we labeled our map:

> **Sheriff**—a plastic sheriff's badge
>
> **Farrier**—a horseshoe
>
> **Farmer**—an ear of corn
>
> **Newspaper editor**—a copy of the classroom newspaper (see page 138)

Activity

9

Pioneer family—a covered wagon (see page 34)

Railroad engineer—a picture of a train

Banker—sample bank notes (see page 15)

(For a sample map and an index to the location of the cowboy, see pages xix–xxii.)

Introduce a lesson about cardinal and intermediate directions. Have the students create a compass rose and place a sample on the map.

Map keys are important features for map reading. Create a key that shows symbols for cities, rivers, mountains, lakes, political boundaries, etc.

Using on-line telecommunications services, plot the daily weather of the cities the Cowboy visits. Post copies of daily weather reports on your classroom bulletin board. Make a graph comparing the weather of your city with the weather of the cities the Cowboy passes through.

Hang copies of all communiqués on the map. We recommend that the letters be hung in three stacks:

* letters from the Cowboy
* letters to the Cowboy
* letters from the characters

Include on the bulletin board any media coverage from community newspapers, school newspapers, and photographs taken throughout the project that shows students in action. The map will become a wonderful documentation of the entire activity.

Letter 3
Preparations Continue

I am preparing for a very exciting adventure that is soon to begin. I know that I will have to use all my skill and knowledge to survive. No doubt I will have to put all my ranching skills to use along the way. Have you ever wondered what a cowboy does with his time?

Cowboys really do rope those cattle. Normally we just "drive" them, herding them in groups. But now and then, one gets into some trouble and if we can't steer it back to the herd, we have to rope it to bring it back. You can't just yell, "Get back over here, little doggie!" Also, when we need to brand them to identify them for a specific owner, we will rope them so we can keep them quiet until we finish the branding. I would imagine that having a hot iron heated over an open fire and then pressed against the skin does hurt, but it has to be done. Any other marking would come off when the hair grew out. Maybe someday ranchers will find some other way to mark the skin so the brand doesn't disappear as the cattle age.

Like anything else, roping takes quite a bit of time and practice to learn. I've been roping since I was a boy. My pa had me rope tree stumps. Tree stumps never move nor pull when you rope 'em. Then I advanced to roping fence posts. Still not too exciting, but what can I say? They were there. I tried to rope our cattle dog, but he was too fast and always acted like we were just playing. Later I worked on a ranch east of the Mississippi where I learned from some real ranchers and farmers about roping.

Kaper King is very light gray with some very small gray and brown spots. But from more than 10 feet away he looks almost white. He is very striking. He has been with me for some time. He is about 17 years old and has seen a lot of country east of the "Big River." Most horses only live to be about 25 years old. Of course, some live longer while others don't. I sure hope he is around for a long time as he has become my best friend.

I'm now making my final preparations for my departure from St. Louis. I had taken all of my money from the town bank in Quincy before I left. The bank issued me what are called "bank notes," which are like local money. I've decided to take the bank notes to the bank here in St. Louis and exchange them for gold coins so that it will be easier for me to buy things while on my journey. I've found that people want money they can feel and see—that's why I'll be carrying gold and gold coins on my trip west. Also, those bank notes can get ruined in the harsh conditions encountered during the trip. Just imagine Kaper King and me going across a deep, raging river and later finding out that all my bank notes got wet and no longer had any value. Even though those coins are heavy, they'll be the best for us.

Well, I see a bank building over on the street corner, so I'm going to go over there to see if I can make the exchange. It sure looks like a fancy place. I'll try to meet the banker and see if he will also write to you. It looks like I will leave St. Louis tomorrow for the journey west. I'll write again soon.

Sincerely from St. Louis,
The Cowboy

Letter from the Banker

My name is James P. Fargo, and I am the respected banker right here in the center of St. Louis. My father opened this institution about 27 years ago. My father has since retired, thus leaving me with the dual responsibilities of serving my customers while making a profit. I have two other employees who work with me: Mr. Sanders, the bank manager, and Miss Peacock, the teller and bookkeeper. The bank building is constructed of fine fired red brick with strong mortar, making for a distinguished-looking corner site in downtown.

We are one of the many private banks opening up as the Western Territory expands. Originally, we borrowed money from a large New England trust company to meet our expenses. Since those early years, we have done well, and our loan is free and clear. Our bank, although starting modestly with just two tables, a file cabinet, a few chairs, and a corner safe, has come a long way. I still remember that grand wooden rolltop desk. As a boy I once climbed right under that cover, and my sister Patricia closed the top on me. Caught my finger in the lid, and you could hear the scream all the way to Colorado.

We still have the original wood-burning stove in the corner, and of course, Mr. Sanders is still with us. He has been with the bank for 25 years. He knows almost everything there is to know about banking. He could take you for a tour of our walk-in vault and show you the gold storage boxes, the document boxes, and even the small safe where the original city charter is kept.

From *Galloping Along the Old West Trails* © 1996 Teacher Ideas Press 1-800-237-6124.

As you probably know, there isn't a national currency, which makes for many problems for both the banker and business. With each private bank issuing its own bank notes, it can be quite confusing, especially if a bank is in business today, but not tomorrow. What this means is that every bank has its own money. It can be a problem if you cash in your mining gold for bank notes and then the bank goes out of business.

Some folks still prefer to keep their money under the mattress or under the cupboard. One old-timer went looking for his money in his straw mattress only to find that some pesky rodents had eaten the stuffing AND all his money. All that was left was some shredded paper resembling the color of our bank notes. Because I remembered the transaction, and we still had the original exchange on the ledgers, we were able to give him new bank notes as replacements. I hope there was a lesson learned. I wish I could say that the bank is the best place to keep one's money, but only last week in Abilene, three bandits robbed the Abilene National of $5,000. I guess there are no guarantees.

The banking business is wonderful. We help by making loans to new businesses, to farmers, and to ranchers. With each loan a dream may come true and our nation gets richer. Banking will probably be one of those businesses that will be around as long as there are people with dreams. The bankers are the true builders of the West. If you should someday be in St. Louis, be sure to stop by the bank. I'll personally show you around.

Sincerely,
James P. Fargo

From *Galloping Along the Old West Trails* © 1996 Teacher Ideas Press   1-800-237-6124.

Activity

In 1857, there was no national bank. As a result, public and private banks in the 29 states printed and distributed their own bank notes.

Bank Notes

Objective

Students will design unique currency for the classroom or school bank.

Materials

* ★ Paper
* ★ Colored pencils, crayons
* ★ Ruler
* ★ Samples of current and historical currency (These can be the real thing or reproductions and photographs found in resources from the library.)

Procedure

In cooperative groups, have the students identify and list ten characteristics found in the sample bills. The students then create one bill of their own design that incorporates the findings of the group.

When designing the note, use today's currency as inspiration. Have the students examine with a magnifying glass a one dollar bill, then list the features they observe. You may want to look at larger denominations, but I'd stick to the smaller denominations, stressing the importance of honesty and trustworthiness. After all, it's your money!

Talk about the people depicted on the bills. Whose picture is found on the one dollar bill, the five dollar bill, the one hundred dollar bill? Are women represented on the currency? Are people of various ethnic backgrounds seen on the bills? Why or why not? Ask the students to select people they would feature on the bills, and tell why.

Compare the value of the dollar in the late 1850s to its value today. List items that could be bought for one dollar (or one hundred dollars) in 1857 and those items that can be bought today.

Following the discussions, have students create their own designs. They may want to select traditional colors or create new concepts for currency. (Check out the newest colors of various crayon-type markers, complete with glitter!) Or maybe they could include a hologram to prevent counterfeiting.

Activity   15

Letter 4
Getting Ready
to Leave St. Louis

Banking and business taken care of, I've strapped tightly to Kaper King's saddle all the supplies that I can carry. I'm finally off on my journey west. I really won't miss the hustle and bustle of St. Louis, although I know some people love the excitement of the big city. I suppose that is what makes this country so great—everyone can find something and somewhere that feels right to them. I guess I haven't found mine yet, which is why I'm headed where I am. This city is so big that Kaper King and I can't see the end of it, but I know we are almost to the outskirts. That's because people are coming from the opposite direction toward the center of town. Most folks probably have a good idea where I'm headed, seeing all the gear on Kaper King. Most of those who pass say things like "Good luck," "Safe journey," "Hope you find what you're looking for," and "I'll be out West too next year." I always say "Thanks" and give them a wave. I smile and shout back jokingly, "I'll save some land for you." They wave back and soon disappear into the city.

As we rode around a corner, I heard the loudest shrill whistle imaginable. Sounded like a teakettle the size of a mountain. Kaper King threw his head up and looked to the left and at the same time jumped sideways. Before us was a huge black iron locomotive with separate cars in tow. It was very still, except for the immense plume of white steam spewing from the top. I had heard the noise from these locomotives before, but only from a distance when I was on the farm.

Getting Ready to Leave St. Louis

From *Galloping Along the Old West Trails* © 1996 Teacher Ideas Press 1-800-237-6124.

Never had I been so close. The giant wheels and connecting bars of steel, the gears, and black paint made it look like the most powerful thing on earth. I always knew that someday these great machines would take people and supplies out West in but a few weeks. Amazing when you think about it. My trip will take months.

One thing I knew for sure, Kaper King and most of the other horses were not too fond of this invention. I've heard it called the "Iron Horse," but certainly Kaper King didn't consider it a horse. Once I got him calmed down, however, he seemed rather curious. I thought this would be a good time to let him get a bit closer. Might as well get him accustomed to it in case we should again be surprised on the trail by such a mighty machine. We rode closer, when suddenly a man wearing a striped shirt and dark pants stepped out from between the locomotive and the fuel car. He said, "Hi, stranger! Sorry to frighten your horse. Seems we always do that until the animal gets used to us. I'm the engineer of the train." I introduced myself and Kaper King. He turned out to be a nice man and had quite a lot to say. I'll write more when I can. I'm really on my way!

Your friends,
The Cowboy and Kaper King

Getting Ready to Leave St. Louis

From *Galloping Along the Old West Trails* © 1996 Teacher Ideas Press 1-800-237-6124.

Letter from the Railroad Engineer

It sure isn't a glamorous job, and certainly not a clean one. You'll never see an engineer of a great locomotive wearing a fancy suit. No, sir, we wear overalls and a hat to protect our skin from the soot and ash from those burning ovens; the heat generated from them will power this mighty engine to help this nation grow.

I'm an engineer for the Pacific Railroad Company in Missouri. It seems like I started with the railroad just a few years ago, and now I am one of the oldest engineers to work the track. I realize, of course, that more and more young engineers are being hired each week. Part of the reason is the many accidents that occur on the new lines being built. You better not let on to the management of the railroad that I'm telling you all of this, but the story must be told. Sometimes we get the feeling that the folks in the main office just want to get those trains rolling at any cost. The faster the rail companies can get rolling, the more land they are able to get from the government. I think their plan is to sell off the extra land and make huge profits. Anyway, just the other day a train carrying 10 cars of passengers and cargo fell through a trestle. The rail company tried to keep it quiet, but a reporter from an eastern paper had a sister on that ill-fated train. He was waiting for her, and when the train was late he began an investigation. That resulted in the story being reported around the territory. I suppose that with greater advances and more attention to detail these kinds of things will decrease. In the meantime, I guess it is up to us, the engineers, to protect our passengers.

I check the line carefully on each run, trying to see up ahead for any problems with the track. Sometimes it can be the weather that loosens a footing of a rail tie, or a landslide that blocks and tears the track. We often put a "point man" right up on the front of the locomotive whose only job is to look far ahead for danger. If he sees anything, he immediately signals the engineer and the brakes come on fast and hard. When these trains are traveling at up to 40 miles an hour, they don't stop quickly.

The hours are long, and the pay isn't great, but I'm helping to open up the new territories and that is important for our young nation. I hope to see you all soon aboard one of my trains. Take care now.

Engineer Brady

From *Galloping Along the Old West Trails*   © 1996   Teacher Ideas Press   1-800-237-6124.

Activities

To some, it was the Iron Horse that forged the West. Tracks connected major cities and growing towns. With the roaring of the engine and the blowing of the whistle, the West became open to anyone willing to make the journey.

Songs of the Railroad

Much of the history of the United States is preserved and passed down through the songs of the period. Teach the students traditional favorites such as "I've Been Working on the Railroad," "John Henry," and "Drill Ye Tarriers, Drill."

Once the children are familiar with the tunes, have them write additional verses. They can then illustrate a classroom book that can be shared with reading buddies or parents. They can even write their own songs.

Build a Bridge

Objective

Students use inquiry and experimentation to design and construct bridges with plastic straws.

Materials

* ★ Plastic straws
* ★ Masking tape
* ★ Scissors

Procedure

Divide the students into groups. Provide each group with plastic straws and a roll of masking tape. Instruct the students to build a bridge that can sustain the weight of a "train." If you have an electric train available with tracks, this would be ideal. If not, use anything heavy to place in the center of the bridge. Provide the children with no other instructions. Ask them if they can discover any special shapes used in the construction of their bridge. Focus on triangles, squares, parallelograms, and rectangles. Are any of these shapes more useful, or do any provide greater strength than others?

Toothpick Race

Once again divide the class into cooperative groups. Provide each group with a box of toothpicks. Go outside to the playground blacktop (or any large paved area) and mark off a 20-foot line. Mark the center of the line with a large X. Position a group at each end of the line. (You may have to make four or five lines depending on the size of your class.) Instruct the students to work carefully but quickly in laying the ties and tracks of the railroad. The toothpicks should be laid parallel to form the outside tracks and crossed perpendicular to create the crossties. The group that reaches the center first is the group that will control the railroad.

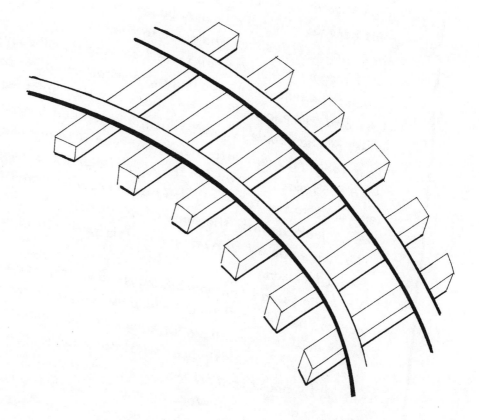

From *Galloping Along the Old West Trails* © 1996 Teacher Ideas Press 1-800-237-6124.

Letter 5
Somewhere Near a Small
Town Down the Trail

Well, I've been riding for what seems like many long days, and I'm ready for a hotel, a hot meal, and a restful night's sleep. I certainly was anxious to get away from that locomotive in St. Louis, though. It made Kaper King and me just a bit nervous. The big city may be exciting, but I still prefer the open range, with space and quiet to think.

I'm coming upon a small town. I can see its silhouette up against the hills as the sun begins to sneak down beneath the horizon. It sure looks like a tiny place but that suits me fine. Most of the people I've met thus far have been friendly and hospitable. As I ride into the main street, it seems like it might be a good place to stay for the night. I didn't see a sign at the entrance to the town, so I don't even know its name. From the way it looks against the sunset, I might call it Sweet Horizon. That would be a fine name for a little town out here. So it is, Sweet Horizon.

I can see a small boardinghouse down the road and a cafe across the street. Although I've only been gone for a bit over a week now, it seems like a lot longer. Maybe someone has a newspaper so I can find out what has been happening back home. I suppose that by the time a newspaper gets here, the news is a month old. Word of mouth is probably the best way to find out what changes are going on back East and in the West. If I ever stay in one place long enough, I'd sure like to get some mail.

Somewhere Near a Small Town Down the Trail

From *Galloping Along the Old West Trails* © 1996 Teacher Ideas Press   1-800-237-6124.

I asked a young bearded fellow in front of the store if he knew where I might put up Kaper King for the night. Needs to be a safe place where he can be out of the cold and get some dry feed. Sometimes those stables give horses bad feed, and by morning you have your best friend rolling on the ground from colic, a killer stomach pain. He told me there is a good stable halfway down the street and just east at the corner. I can see it now. Looks good. I'll find that stable keeper and see if he can put Kaper King up for the night. Then, off I go to the boardinghouse for a good meal and warm bath.

I'll write to you just as soon as I can. I never know if the stage line or private horse riders will get this mail to you, but I'm hoping so.

Your friends,
The Cowboy and
Kaper King

P.S. I may be looking for a little work on a ranch or a cattle drive to help stretch out my money. I found a posting in the newspaper. I'll let you know if anything comes of it.

Letter from the Stable Keeper

What once was the last building in town now is somewhere just south of the center. Our small town is growing so fast as more and more settlers move west. They often stop here for necessary repairs to their wagons or to get a night's sleep, a hot bath, or even some entertainment. We get families traveling alone or with the wagon trains, outlaws, explorers, and lonesome cowboys. We even had a group of English gentlemen thinking they could find a proper fox hunt. Never did hear from that group again. Whatever the reason, most folks need a place to leave their horses for the night. On occasion a stranger will leave his horse for a couple of hours and just never return. I have them pay up front, but if they don't return, I'm forced to sell the horse and other belongings left behind. I wonder what becomes of those travelers.

Yes, I am the Stable Keeper. We provide shelter for the horses and some good grain after many weeks on the trail. Most of the horses graze along the way and keep fairly healthy. On occasion, however, they're worked too hard and ridden too long and are nothing but a bag of bones. A horse is your best friend out on the prairie. You treat 'em well and they will take care of you. I had this cowboy come through here not too long ago who had this fine horse. His name was . . . can't quite remember the whole name but had the word King in it. He treated that animal like a king, that's for sure. You could tell they were best friends. Those two will be all right out there on the plains.

Some horsemen just want a place to get their horses out of the weather; others want extra grain, some grooming, and some care. One cowboy told me to keep his horse through the spring until she (the mare that is) had her foal. He gave me $20 to cover the expenses. She had a fine baby. I have them both out back as he never did return. Couldn't part with those two. It's been nearly a year now.

If you were here, you'd notice the pump near the entrance, then you'd know how fortunate I am to have a well under my property. These horses often drink 20 to 30 gallons a day. That would be a lot of water to carry. A good stable keeper ensures that the place is clean and free from diseases. No cowboy wants to leave a horse where it might get sick. So the manure needs to be cleaned out every day! I sometimes hire some of the town kids as stable boys to clean out the stalls and pens. We use a large manure fork and a shovel. As often as possible, I take in an orphan boy to sleep here at night and watch out for sick horses or possible thieves. As well, we always have to be on the alert for fire. With all the hay and straw bedding, fire is the greatest fear. I'm always looking for good help. Seems like just when I get someone good, he gets the urge to go farther west.

Well, if any of you find yourselves heading through our town, look in on me. There is always something to do. This is one job where the work just keeps piling up.

If you see that cowboy on the horse, give him my regards.

Best to you,
D. Peters

From *Galloping Along the Old West Trails* © 1996 Teacher Ideas Press 1-800-237-6124.

Activity

Kaper King isn't just a horse. He is a mathematical four-legged equine, just as sure as water flows downhill! Just picture this fine beast. He is bigger than a tumbleweed and longer than a coyote. He can travel many miles in a day and eats according to his size, weight, and level of activity. He is symmetrical, too! What does all this really mean? Kaper King, just like the rest of the world, is Mathematical! Let's find out more.

The following activity provides some out-of-the-ordinary applications for daily math skills. How many of us have ever made calculations based on a horse? Use all the tools of math—calculators, rulers, pencils, paper—and, of course, your minds.

Figuring Out Horses

Objective

Students solve math problems.

Materials

* ★ Activity sheets (see pages 27–28)
* ★ G&S Tack Emporium spring catalog (see page 29)
* ★ Ruler
* ★ Calculator
* ★ Pencil

Procedure

Circulate among students as they work individually, with partners, or in small groups to "figure out" horses.

Find the Height of a Horse

The height of a horse is usually measured in "hands"; this comes from the time when the measuring device was a human hand. A hand is considered to be the width of a man's hand, or 4 inches.

Find the measurements in hands for the horses of the followng sizes:

63 inches = _____ hands

55 inches = _____ hands

52 inches = _____ hands

Find the height in inches for horses of the following sizes:

14 hands = _____ inches

16 hands = _____ inches

13 hands = _____ inches

Ask the Cowboy for the hand measurement for Kaper King. Convert it to inches.

Kaper King is _____ hands. He is _____ inches tall.

Feeding a Horse

The following table is a good guide for the average horse.

Daily Performance	Hay
0–1 hours light work	1 flake* twice a day
1–2 hours average work	1½ flakes twice a day
3–4 hours average work or 2 hours hard work	1 flake three times a day

*A flake weighs about 8 pounds

Calculate the amount of food required for the following horses:

★ an 800-pound pony used for light work 2 hours a day

★ a 1,000-pound horse turned out to pasture (no work)

★ a 1,200-pound horse used for 3–4 hours of average work

The best advice is this: If the horse gains weight and starts looking chubby, cut back the food just a bit. If it looks skinny or is working harder, give it a bit more. Observe your horse daily and don't make any large feed changes.

Ask the Cowboy how much Kaper King weighs. Find out Kaper King's daily activities. Based on this information, calculate the amount of food he must be fed.

Weight of Kaper King _____

Daily activity _____

Hay requirements _____

From *Galloping Along the Old West Trails* © 1996 Teacher Ideas Press 1-800-237-6124.

Feeding Costs

Now that you know how much to feed a horse, you need to know how much it will cost.

Hay is usually sold by the bale. Alfalfa hay sells for $9 a bale during the summer. A bale of hay weighs nearly 100 pounds. A flake weighs about 8 pounds. There are 12 flakes to a bale.

Using the above information, figure the daily, weekly, monthly, and yearly costs to feed Kaper King. Show your work and explain how you reached these numbers.

Daily cost $ _____

Weekly cost $ _____

Monthly cost $ _____

Yearly cost $ _____

A Home for Kaper King

Any horse owner knows that a horse needs shelter from the weather; a small barn works best. In addition to a place to shelter the horse, the owner also needs a place to groom the horse and store his tack and feed.

The Cowboy has asked you to design a home for Kaper King. Using the scale 1 inch equals 1 foot, design a basic stable floor plan with the following features:

    ✶ 2 stalls, each 12 feet by 14 feet

    ✶ Tack room, 10 feet by 12 feet

    ✶ Feed room, 12 feet by 12 feet

    ✶ Extra hay storage, 10 feet by 10 feet

Draw your design on a separate peice of paper. Write a paragraph explaining your design.

Equipping a Horse

Using the following catalog page, selected the basic Western tack you would need for riding a horse. You have a maximum of $1,200 to spend. (What's a "tack" anyway?)

List the item, price and total below:

Saddle $_____

Bridle $_____

Blanket/Pad $_____

Other $_____

Total $_____

From *Galloping Along the Old West Trails* © 1996 Teacher Ideas Press 1-800-237-6124.

G&S Tack Emporium

Spring Catalog

Western Saddle

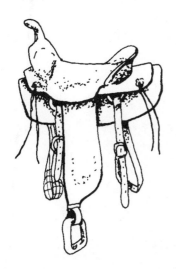

16-inch seat, full rigging
Brown finish
Price $21.82
Shipping weight 31 lbs.

Fleece Saddle Pad

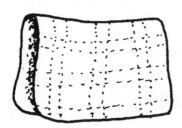

30 × 30 inches, washable
Available in red,
blue, or green
Price $0.90
Shipping weight 4 lbs.

Sterling Quality Outstanding Value

West Texas Rider

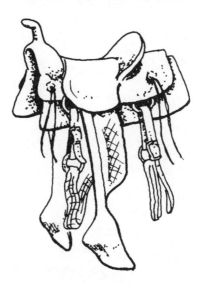

16-inch seat,
3-inch cantle
Price $26.90
Available with
stirrup tooling, $31.85
Shipping weight 36 lbs.

Shipping charges:
$1.00 per $100.00 of purchase

Browband Bridle

5/8-inch latigo, brown,
grazing bit
Price $1.95
Shipping weight 3 lbs.

One-Ear Bridle

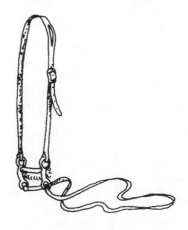

1/2-inch latigo,
Curb bit
Tan Price $2.85
Brown Price $2.85
Shipping weight 3 lbs.

From *Galloping Along the Old West Trails* © 1996   Teacher Ideas Press   1-800-237-6124.

Letter 6
Somewhere Near Kansas,
Almost to the Shawnee Trail

Last night was cold, but the stars were bright and bold. The wind was still, and each of the bright lights in the sky seemed to speak to me in a soft voice. I sure wonder what those bright lights really are. Some say they are guiding lights for travelers like me. Others say they are magnificent molten suns, like the sun that shines on the earth. Still others say they are planets like ours, reflecting in the darkness. That might be a good question for some of you to look into. If you find anything out, let me know.

I awoke this morning and met up with a pioneer family. They were nice people and had some good stories to tell. These are the kind of people who are making the territories strong. I'll ask them to send you a letter and share what it is like to be a pioneer family in the 1850s.

I will be heading south soon, possibly to take a job with the Kallenbauch family. They are the ones who put the advertisement in the paper for a cowhand. I told them I would contact them when I got a bit closer. Should be near a town in a day or so, and will contact them from the telegraph office. I'll write more soon. Keep an eye out for a clear trail wherever you travel. Keep smiling!

Your friend
(a little cold this morning),
The Cowboy

From *Galloping Along the Old West Trails* © 1996 Teacher Ideas Press 1-800-237-6124.

*Letter from the
Pioneer Family*

My name is Emily Castle, and it has been nearly 12 weeks since we left Missouri. I can remember waiting in town for the wagon train to assemble and a trail boss to be assigned to our group. We were all so excited to be leaving. Now, many months later and fewer of us still moving west, the days are long and hard. Most of the people, except for the very young and the very old, spend a good part of the day walking alongside the wagons. We stop each evening and reassess our supplies and raise our spirits for the adventure of the coming days and weeks. I remember when the wagons were new and the canvas covers were still a clean beige. After so many weeks of the hot sun, wind, dust, and afternoon rain showers, many are tattered, mud caked, and torn.

Two weeks ago, we decided that with our wagon breaking up and supplies scarce, we would settle here on the western plains. We waved good-bye to the folks continuing west. It was sad to realize that our original dream would not come true … at least for now. We scouted around for a site to call our camp and James, my husband, went looking for materials to build a fine home. There are so few trees that building out of mud or below the level of the rolling hills seems to be the most efficient way of making a shelter. We haven't decided whether this will be our final stop, but for at least this year and possibly next, we shall call this place home. A couple of other families also decided to settle here as the trip just has become too difficult. We still have our strength, and this is essential for building and starting our settlement. James and I are breaking up the hard soil with help from the wagon horses and the light plow purchased in St. Louis. Our daughter,

From *Galloping Along the Old West Trails* © 1996 Teacher Ideas Press 1-800-237-6124.

Charlotte, and I prepare the meals and keep some order to what we are doing. Our son, Kevin, watches over our small animals and tries to stay out of trouble. If all goes well, we will be planting our small garden first and then more crops later. We must raise enough food from the land to sustain us and the animals for the next year. We will have no new clothes for a long time, so the ladies will mend and sew as the need arises.

The days are long, but this is our home, and we feel good as the day turns to night. Often the other families stop by and we talk and share our progress. If anyone gets in trouble, the other families are there to help. That is the way of the West. We pray that no one will become seriously ill. We heard stories of people just over the hill dying from a fast moving fever. I hope God will guide us through this difficult time. We must have faith, but the hard work for survival will be ours.

I know we can make it through this year.

My love from the Plains,
Emily

Letter from the Pioneer Family

From *Galloping Along the Old West Trails* © 1996 Teacher Ideas Press   1-800-237-6124.

Activities

From a distant grassy knoll, we looked out to see a line of white-sailed schooners rising and falling upon the waves of the endless prairie.

Westward ho! Land rushes, gold rushes, and the pioneer spirit guided the hopes and dreams of the western adventurer. With its canvas rippling in the wind and rickety wheels turning, the Conestoga wagon became the symbol of undaunting courage and the hope for an expanding nation.

Covered Wagon #1

Objective
The students will make replicas of the Conestoga wagon.

Materials

★ Wooden tongue depressors, toothpicks

★ Newsprint, tagboard, brown construction paper

★ Scissors, glue

Procedure

Give each child four wooden tongue depressors, along with the other materials listed above. Place tagboard on a tabletop. Arrange the four tongue depressors on the board so that they are parallel to each other with the edges touching. Glue them to the tagboard.

To create the canvas top, fold the newsprint horizontally in half. Crinkle fold and pinch the lower edges until they fit the top edge of the row of tongue depressors. Gently billow the paper to create the look of a canvas top.

Next, cut two 3" circles from the brown construction paper. To create the look of wagon spokes, arrange and glue toothpicks in a crisscross pattern on the paper wheels. Position the wheels beneath the low portion of the buckboard and glue them in place.

When the glue has completely dried, trim away any excess tagboard. Have your students draw or trace oxen or horses to pull their wagons. (You can also use commercial die patterns for oxen, mules, horses, etc., if available at your district resource center.)

Figure 6.1 illustrates a completed wagon.

From *Galloping Along the Old West Trails*   © 1996   Teacher Ideas Press   1-800-237-6124.

FIGURE 6.1 COVERED WAGON #1

Activities

Covered Wagon #2

Objective

Students will construct a three-dimensional covered wagon.

Materials

★ Newsprint, brown construction paper, tagboard, or heavy cardboard

★ Wooden tongue depressors, pipe cleaners

★ Muslin

★ Scissors, glue

Procedure

Using an old shoe box for the buckboard, have the students cover the outside with brown construction paper or wooden tongue depressors to create the look of wood. Wagon wheels can be made of heavy tagboard or cardboard.

The size of the wagon wheels will vary depending on the size of the shoe box. Cut four wheels of appropriate size from the cardboard. Decorate with construction paper or toothpicks to create wagon spokes. Turn box on its side and glue down two wheels. Half of the wheel should touch the side of the box and the other half should extend beyond the box. Flip the box over to the other side and repeat. Let dry overnight. In the morning, set the box upright on all four wheels.

The wagon bows can be created using 12-inch pipe cleaners. Distribute 5 pipe cleaners to each student. Bend to form the bows of the wagon. Attach to the side of the wagon with tape, then reinforce with a staple or two. Remember that the bows should be distributed evenly, perhaps 1 or 2 inches apart.

To create the canvas top, spread of thin layer of glue on each pipe cleaner. Carefully position a piece of muslin cut to the right size and attach it to the top of the bows. Let dry overnight.

If you need a team of animals for the display, try borrowing someone's plastic horse (or oxen) collection.

Bidding Adieu

Families packed their bags, loaded their wagons, and kissed their loved ones good-bye. The journey before them was long and often tortuous. Few knew what their future would hold. Still, they forged west with the hope for a better life on the new frontier. Explore with students the following aspects of the trek west.

What to take. When pioneer families moved west, they packed everything they could carry into the wagon (kind of like a sixth grader going on an overnighter). Anything that wouldn't fit was left behind. Ask students to think about what they would do if they were in a similar situation. Have them think about what they would take and what they would leave behind. How would they prioritize their choices? Would monetary value or sentimental value play the major role in the final selection of what items to take?

Letters home. Writing letters was one of the few ways to keep in touch with the folks back home. However, the mail was slow and unreliable. It was not unusual for mail to take up to six months to reach its destination, and many letters never arrived. The pioneers' handwritten pages were packed with information of their new lives and stories of their travels. Review with students the format for a friendly letter, then have them write letters, either to someone they have not written to in a long time, or as a make-believe pioneer detailing his or her experiences along the trail to loved ones back home.

Journals. Much of what we know of the pioneer experience was recorded in the journal entries made by those making the journey. Their experiences and personal perceptions were preserved for historians and students alike. Have the students keep a daily journal. Let them react to the letters of the Cowboy and the other characters they encounter out west.

Little Cabins on the Prairie

Laura Ingalls Wilder's books about pioneer life are among the most beloved of children's stories. In *Little House on the Prairie*, the author describes the building and construction of the family's cabin.

Objective

The students will build an original log cabin using a variety of building materials, depending on the student's creativity.

Materials

* Pretzels
* Ice cream sticks
* Twigs
* Cereal
* Clay
* Cinnamon sticks
* Straws
* Graham crackers

Procedure

This lesson is designed to be done at home. Inform the students that they can build a log cabin out of any chosen material but that manufactured building blocks are not to be used. The cabin should be built on a base no larger than 12 by 12 inches. (If you don't specify a size restriction, some students will be tempted to build structures large enough to be called "The Staff Lounge.") Instruct the students to follow these steps in completing this activity:

1. Design a floor plan.
2. Make a list of the materials to be used.
3. Make an outline of the steps that will be followed in building the cabin.
4. Build the cabin according to the plans formulated in steps 1–3.

Allow students plenty of time (and at least a couple of weekends) to complete the project. Encourage parents to assist their children but not to do the project for them. (This is not a parent competitive project.) Be prepared to see the greatest array of "log cabins" ever to grace the cybertrail. Some may look like gingerbread houses, complete with gumdrops and white icing. Others will look like the real McCoy!

Letter 7
Heading South
on the Shawnee Trail

I'm still planning on taking that job (at least for a short while) with the Kallenbauch family in Kansas. When Kaper King and I get to the next town, we'll see if we can find a telegraph office and send a message to the family. It would be nice to settle in for a while and get real cleaned up, be warm for a few nights, and even mend a few of my things that need fixing. My riding chaps were torn in the right leg when they got caught on some old sharp brushwood. I really need to get those fixed before I begin to drive cattle. Also, my spurs got bent sideways and need some metalwork. You might want to find out more about some of the clothing that cowboys wear when doing different kinds of jobs. Feel free to write to me and ask questions or tell me what you learned.

There's that town up ahead now. I'll just go on down the main street. Looks like there's a telegraph office across from the U.S. Marshall's office. I think I'll go in and send off that telegraph to the Kallenbauch family regarding the job offer. Will write to you all soon.

Your friend,
The Cowboy

P.S. I attached a copy of the telegram I sent to Mr. Kallenbauch.

WESTERN UNION TELEGRAPH COMPANY

MR. KALLENBAUCH
NEAR WICHITA STATION
TELEGRAPH FALL 1857
FROM COWBOY LOOKING FOR WORK

MR. KALLENBAUCH AND FAMILY STOP NOW HERE NEAR
YOUR RANCH AND WOULD STILL LIKE TO WORK IF JOB
IS OPEN STOP WOULD BE WILLING TO DO MOST
ANYTHING INCLUDING DRIVING THE CATTLE SOUTH AND
THEN NORTH STOP I AM IN TOWN NOW AND WILL BE AT
THE HOTEL FOR THREE DAYS OR UNTIL I HEAR FROM
YOU STOP THANK YOU STOP END

From *Galloping Along the Old West Trails*   © 1996   Teacher Ideas Press   1-800-237-6124.

My name is Robert P. Montgomery, and I work for the Western Union Telegraph Company, by far the largest telegraph company in the country. This company just didn't grow this big overnight. No, it was the hard work of dedicated business people who combined 12 other companies to form Western Union. Of course, you understand that sending messages and communicating with people is even more important now that the country is expanding. Telegraph is almost as fast as the spoken word. It can transfer messages in what took weeks and sometimes months in only minutes. It wasn't too long ago that the Pony Express was bringing letters and messages across the territories on the fastest horses with the most experienced riders. That didn't last long because soon we could get the same message in an instant anywhere that the wire could stretch, at a lot cheaper price.

This is how it all works. I have an office down on the main street of town. Someone who wants to send a message comes to the office. I count up the words and change the words into a special code designed by Samuel Morse. I click out the

Letter from the Telegraph Operator

From *Galloping Along the Old West Trails* © 1996 Teacher Ideas Press 1-800-237-6124.

code on this little key machine, and it sends electrical signals through the wire. Another operator somewhere down the line hears the clicking and changes it back to letters and words. What a great system! Of course, the system only works if we have electricity running through those wires. It's difficult to understand, but it works.

The folks back at Western Union in St. Louis say that the signals that I send through the wire move at the speed of 186,282 miles a second. That's faster than any horse and rider I know! Anyway, when I receive messages, I decode them and write them out on lined paper. I usually have a young boy or assistant deliver the messages on horseback or by horse and wagon. I guess someday every town will have a telegraph office. Who knows, people may be able to send messages from California to New York. Some fools even think we will be able to send pictures through those little wires!

My wife, Jane, called down and said lunch is ready NOW! Well, even the telegraph operator gets hungry. What do you think about the future of the telegraph? You all take care.

Yours truly,
Robert Montgomery

Letter from the Telegraph Operator   41

Activities

When we imagine the Wild West, saloons, gunfights, and the Pony Express come to mind. We see that brave rider galloping over the barren plains, changing horses and courier bags only to ride off again to the next station. (Note that you never see them sip a cup of water, eat a hearty meal, or relieve themselves!) Although this may be a deep-rooted image of the West, the truth is that the Pony Express was short-lived, lasting a mere nine months. The advent of the telegraph changed the information highway from a dusty trail to wire strung from pole to pole.

String That Wire

Samuel Morse first devised a signaling code in 1838. Composed of two characters (the dash and the dot), its varied combinations of symbols represented letters and numerals. When combined with an electromagnet receiver, the pulse of the current from the sender would deflect a soft iron armature attached to a magnet. A pencil attached to the armature would record the dots and dashes on a strip of paper, which would then be decoded by the telegraph operator.

Discuss with students the history of the telegraph, Samuel Morse, and the code that bears his name. Look at the importance of this invention for long-distance communication. Compare communication of yesterday with that of today's high technology. Understand the role the telegraph played in the opening of the West.

Have students write their own messages in Morse code. Working in pairs, have the students send messages back and forth. Write the code on paper, send messages to friends across the hall, or tap the code on a wall. (Be sure not to disturb the teacher next door unless it's a rainy day and you are tapping an SOS.)

The Information Pioneer

Available to the educator and student of today is a vast resource of computer technology. Commercial computer programs specifically designed for children can provide new and exciting avenues for learning. The technology can be easily integrated into all areas of your curriculum. Through the use of computer technology (e.g., telecommunications, CD-ROM, word processing programs, draw programs, and special education enhancement programs) the children will explore history, conduct research, problem solve, demonstrate learning, illustrate stories, and create visual and audio presentations.

As our class journeyed along the Old Cybertrail, the children used a variety of commercial computer programs that enhanced their understanding of the history being studied. Here are just a few:

Wyatt Earp and the Wild West. Take your students on a tour of an old western town and learn about the people who were part of it with this very informative CD-ROM. Although it does have a shoot-out game, you can shut it off. Great for looking into all the buildings of a traditional western town. Features accompanying background music.

Oregon Trail. Our Cowboy traveled along the Oregon Cybertrail on his trek west. The commercial program Oregon Trail enables children to experience life on the frontier and the many hardships and obstacles the settlers faced along the way. As the students travel the trail, they meet people along the way who provide insight and historical perspective. The children must solve problems, challenge the elements to survive, and make decisions that affect their journey west. It is an outstanding simulation that offers great independence and opportunity for problem solving and decision making in a unique western format. Oregon Trail is available in CD-ROM and is a great improvement over the original.

KidPix. KidPix is a computer program that enables the students to become artists. We used KidPix to develop a language arts project. The students were each assigned to read a chapter in *Little House on the Prairie*. They were then responsible for drawing a picture, using KidPix, that represented a scene from the chapter. Once all the pictures were completed, the images were compiled into a computer-generated slide show (another feature of the program). Each student wrote a short narration to accompany his or her original picture, then recorded it using a microphone (very easy to do). The final project was presented on a TV monitor that was attached to the computer. A truly spectacular language arts presentation with an exciting new approach! This program offers great creativity and many applications.

On-line services. With a computer, modem, and your telephone, you and your class can travel and explore the most exciting trail the imagination can offer. Your students can be true pioneers of the Information Communication Frontier whether you are connecting to schools around the corner or research institutes around the world. It is you, the teacher, who possesses the key!

Letter 8
In Town, Waiting for
the Kallenbauch Family

I hope you have heard from some of the interesting and special people I have been meeting along the trail. Let me know. I'm waiting here in town for the Kallenbauch family. I received a telegraph message from them yesterday, and they should be here tomorrow. They informed me they have five children. Sure looking forward to meeting that little herd of kids. Since I wrote to you, I have explored the town, and it's a nice place to spend a few days. Some people will actually live right here for their entire lives. That's a thought, isn't it. I had a wonderful hot meal at the restaurant across the street from the hotel. The proprietor really works hard at making the customers happy. It is such a busy place. People keep coming and going, passing through town on their way west, or while working the cattle drives on the Shawnee or Chisholm Trails. Those are the main trails to get the cattle up or down, to or from, San Antonio. I checked in at the U.S. Marshall's office to see if he could give me more information about the territories that

I would be traveling. The Marshall has a wider jurisdiction than the town sheriff. Both have important jobs. Hope you can meet with them someday. If I get a chance, I'll ask them to write to you.

In the meantime, I will be waiting for Mr. Kallenbauch. I hope he arrives soon. I'll write again from the ranch when I get there. Kaper King says "Hi" ... or whatever horses say!

Your friend,
The Cowboy

In Town, Waiting for the Kallenbauch Family

From *Galloping Along the Old West Trails* © 1996 Teacher Ideas Press 1-800-237-6124.

Letter 9
On the Kallenbauch
Ranch

Just a short note to let you know that I'm settled in at the Kallenbauch Ranch, where I'll be working for a few weeks maybe driving some cattle south and then north on the Shawnee and Chisholm Trails.

I arrived here at the ranch late in the day after Mr. Kallenbauch and little Lori met me in town. The first thing I did was to ask one of the ranch hands where I was to put up Kaper King. He pointed to a rickety old beat-up, fallen-down corral with nails sticking out of the sides. It took me less time than a drop of water coming out of a well tap hittin' the ground to say "Whoa!"

"Not over there, sir." I said. Mr. Kallenbauch and one of the kids overheard me and said, "What's the problem, cowboy?" I shared with him my concern about that old corral and reminded him of the telegram where we talked about good shelter for my horse. I looked yonder to that nice barn and said, "That barn looks great for Kaper King." Mr. Kallenbauch said, "I'm not sure such a fine large horse like yours will fit in our barn stalls." Just then, one of those cute little children asked me how tall and heavy Kaper King was. I explained to that little half pint (the child, not Mr. Kallenbauch) that he is "16 hands." I took great pains to state that those were adult hands, not those of a child. I also told her that he weighed about 1,200 pounds (not that I've ever picked him up and held

On the Kallenbauch Ranch

Galloping Along the Old West Trails © 1996   Teacher Ideas Press   1-800-237-6124.

him on the scales). I told her that I would show her how to measure and weigh a horse without actually picking it up off the ground. She looked at me with wide eyes in amazement. I said, "You just wait a day or two, young lady, and I'll show you how to do it." She smiled and ran off into the family ranch house.

Anyway, we moved Kaper King into the barn, and he fit real nice. He was very happy there too, next to a pretty bay mare. Mr. Kallenbauch gave both of them a handful of oats, alfalfa, and fresh, cool water. They seemed quite content.

I was soon shown to the bunkhouse, which would be my home while working around the ranch and until the cattle drive starts. That's it for tonight. Hope to hear from you soon.

Your friend,
The Cowboy

Galloping Along the Old West Trails © 1996 Teacher Ideas Press 1-800-237-6124

Letter from the Pioneer Child

My name is Lori Kallenbauch. I am nine years old and I live in Wichita, Kansas. The reason I know about you all is because Pa and I picked up a cowboy and his horse, Kaper King, today from town. On our 20-minute ride home, the cowboy told me some great stories. He's really interesting. Anyway, he will be with us for a while. Pa has hired him to rope and brand our cattle when they are driven up from Texas by way of the Chisholm Trail.

Let me tell you something about my life. Pa says that Kansas is pretty much flat with some rolling hills and lots of sunflowers everywhere! Can't say I've seen much else. I live in a house that is called a soddie. That's because it is made out of the earth. When my family and I first arrived here, we dug rectangular blocks of dirt from the ground and stacked them on top of each other to make our house. Pa says that when we have enough money from raising and driving cattle we will build a wood-framed house like our barn. (The barn was built later, when Pa had a chance to order the wood from town.) But for right now there certainly isn't enough money.

I go to school in town normally except when it's either planting time for our personal crops, harvest time, or when the cattle drive comes through. My sisters and brother also help on the ranch doing whatever Pa tells us to do.

I miss school when I'm away, but important work on the ranch must be done. Miss Lumbert is our teacher, and she is really nice. She lets me borrow her private books. I love the stories of faraway places. Before Miss Lumbert

Letter from the Pioneer Child

came to our school we had a teacher who was very stern. I remember once, when I was reciting my English lesson, I got an answer to a question wrong and the teacher slapped my hand with her ruler. My, did that hurt! I also felt so embarrassed. Sometimes we don't have enough slates and the younger children, like my little sisters, have to do their letters and sentences in the dirt on the schoolroom floor. It's much easier to do it on the slates.

I don't have a lot of time to play because there is so much work on the ranch. Every day I gather the eggs, feed the chickens, and pick wild nuts, berries, and seeds (from the sunflowers). Then Ma has me go out to the garden and pick the vegetables that she needs for dinner. My oldest brother brings in the water and the firewood, and if Ma is going to cook meat, we have to go to the meat locker on the side of the house. Ma makes three meals a day. When she's not cooking, she has me help her fill the lamps with oil, clean the house, and wash the clothes on the washboard. Because we don't have any way of storing our fruits and vegetables, Ma says we have to can them. This usually takes half the day!

When I am not working or doing homework, I like playing with my doll, which I made out of a corncob. Someday my Pa is going to build us a seesaw. I can't wait! Well, the oil in my lamp is almost gone and soon I won't have any light to write by, so I better go for now. Write me when you all have some time.

Lori

Letter from the Pioneer Child   49

Activities

Children never really change. They love a good time, to be entertained and have a special treat that is soooooo sweet! It is also universal, for both girls and boys, to find true pleasure in new and adventurous toys.

Introduce traditional delights to your students. They might be surprised by how much they enjoy a piece of homemade taffy or the fun of an old-fashioned game.

Making Taffy

This is a fun (and tasty!) activity that can be done at home or at school. In the classroom, let the students participate in the mixing of ingredients and the taffy pulling. But handle all cooking-related aspects yourself, making sure to keep the students at a safe distance from the heating element.

Ingredients

1 cup sugar	1 tablespoon cornstarch
3/4 cup corn syrup	3 tablespoons butter
2/3 cup water	2 teaspoons vanilla

Procedure

Mix sugar, corn syrup, water, cornstarch, and butter in a saucepan. Without stirring, boil over medium heat to 260 degrees. Remove saucepan from heat and stir in vanilla. Pour contents into a buttered pan. When cool enough to touch, butter the students' hands and have them start pulling the candy until it becomes satiny in appearance and stiff in texture. Cut bite-sized pieces with sterilized scissors and wrap in waxed paper. Commercial flavors can be added in place of the vanilla.

Making Horehound Candy

Another yummy activity that can be done easily in the classroom—provided you follow the caveats outlined in the Making Taffy activity.

Ingredients

2 quarts horehound liquid	1 tablespoon butter
4 cups sugar	1 teaspoon cream of tartar
1 1/4 cups dark corn syrup	

Procedure

To make horehound liquid: Boil 8 cups of water and 1 1/2 quarts loosely packed horehound leaves and stems. Steep, covered, for 20 minutes. Save the liquid, drain and discard the leaves and stems.

Mix remaining ingredients with the horehound liquid and cook over medium heat to 300 degrees. Skim off any top sediment. Pour into a buttered pan. When partially set, score into pieces. Delicious!

Games to Play

When you ask your students today what games they play, they will probably answer with "Nintendo," or "Street Fighter II," or some other handheld, electric-powered toy. Let them have fun learning these traditional favorites:

Jump rope. As the rope twirls, have the kids chant silly little poems they have written in class.

Jacks. This is a good hand-eye coordination game. The first round, let the ball bounce and pick up one jack at a time; the next round, pick up two jacks with each bounce, and so on.

Hopscotch. Great for practicing jumping on one leg or two. The children toss a stone into a formation of squares outlined with chalk on the ground. They then hop through the formation and back again to regain the object.

Tag. Run, chase, touch, you're out! No shoving, we don't want skinned knees.

Hide-and-seek. If they hide too well, the game could be renamed "Ditching School."

Activities

Letter 10
A Few Minutes Alone in
the Morning Sun

Early this morning, Kaper King and I went off alone into the green hills far and above the ranch. It is so quiet and beautiful up here today. When we started out, I could feel the morning mist on my brow, but now the emerging sunshine is beginning to warm us as we ride along. I was to check some of the outer fencing for holes. Not all of the ranch has fencing, but where the water was sour, or where the cattle might wander off and get into danger, Mr. Kallenbauch would fence. I was to repair what I could and mark on my ranch map anything else that needed attention. This was a good way to get to know the layout of the ranch.

The Kallenbauch family are wonderful people. They are loving to each other and good to the ranch hands. Everyone seems to be happy working here. I know it will be difficult to leave as I have become quite attached to the children. They often come out to visit, and we tell stories and laugh. It has been a good time.

As I was riding back to the ranch I spotted out of the corner of my eye some little critter tangled up in the fence near the sagebrush. Actually Kaper King noticed first and threw his head up and drew his ears back. Well, weren't we surprised to find ourselves a sad-looking, brown-eyed golden dog. I reached behind me and got my wire cutters, slid off my saddle, and walked slowly over to this scared fellow. Just clipped a few barbs and free he was. Oops, he's not a he, he's a

From *Galloping Along the Old West Trails* © 1996 Teacher Ideas Press 1-800-237-6124.

she. She slid right up to my leg and started rubbing against me, wagging her tail and licking me on the hand. I think Kaper King and I just found a new friend. Heard some folks from Mexico once call the jagged mountains running north and south the Sierras. I'll call this dog, caught up in that jagged wire, Sierra. Off we went, Kaper King at a slow trot and Sierra running along beside us. Will write soon.

Your friend on a hill
in the morning sun!
The Cowboy

A Few Minutes Alone in the Morning Sun

Letter 11
Headed Down the Shawnee
Trail to San Antonio

We left the Kallenbauch ranch late last week and have been driving cattle down the Shawnee Trail for what seems like 18-hour workdays. We do have to rest the cattle on a regular schedule or they will lose too much weight and won't be worth much when we either get them to market or back to the ranch. So, it's important that we take our time and let the big critters graze along the way. They should be gaining as much weight as they lose, or we'll just have a pack of bones when we get to the end of the cattle drive. That wouldn't be good for anyone. Real cowboys know this and carefully plan the route to be taken and the length of time required to reach the destination.

Sometimes things don't always go as planned. I remember one of the other cowhands telling me that it rained for days and days, and they had to keep those cattle moving or they would lose them in the rising waters. It was hard to tell a steer from a rock because everyone and everything was covered with thick, brown, gooey mud. Another time, the snows came down on the herd way ahead of season, and if the cowhands hadn't kept things moving, the cattle would have froze to death right on the trail. Then there was the time when the river was too high and there was no place to cross, so they had to wait almost two weeks to get to the other side. They had to keep the cattle moving up and down the river to find enough for them all to eat. I wish I had a drawing to show you. Maybe you can imagine what it must have been like.

From *Galloping Along the Old West Trails* © 1996 Teacher Ideas Press 1-800-237-6124.

I'll tell you one thing. You sure do get to know your trail crew—the other cowboys that you ride with. One of the most important people on the trail crew is the trail cook. If the food is good, the cowboys are happy. If the food is bad, you've got sick people everywhere, and the job doesn't get done. Maybe "Cookie," as we call him, will tell you some of the secrets of cooking on the trail. I'll ask him to write.

It's almost the end of the day now, and I'm getting plenty hungry. We've driven the cattle nearly 20 miles today, and I guess it's time for everyone to rest for a while. I can smell the evening meal as the smoke is blowing across our small encampment. The sun will soon be going down, as the days are getting shorter. Winter will soon be upon us. Take care, you little cowpokes.

Your friend,
The Cowboy

Headed Down the Shawnee Trail to San Antonio

Letter from the Trail Cook

Cattle are tough to work, and the cowboy has a rough job for sure, but there ain't no more important job than mine. I'm the Trail Cook and anyone that criticizes my food can just wander off and eat beetles and grubs. I'll keep that trail crew happy with my hearty meals. I've heard stories where a whole trail crew died right during dinner because the trail cook served them spoiled meat. Forty good men and two dogs were buried right where they fell around the evening campfire. Anyone comments about my food and I just remind them of that bunch.

Well, let me just tell you what the life of the trail cook is all about. Me and the other cook hands have to pack the wagon with all the food, supplies, cooking equipment, fresh water, and our personal items for the long cattle drives to the north or west. Sometimes we go out ahead in the morning so that when the herd arrives at the destination for the day, we are nearly ready to serve up food to the crew. At other times, we don't go out ahead, especially if we're heading into uncharted territory. I'm not getting shot just so that a bunch of roughneck cowboys can rub their stomachs. No sir, they will just have to wait until we're good and ready.

One of the most popular meals we serve is beef stew, potatoes, corn, and onions. Sometimes we serve slabs of beef or ribs cooked

From *Galloping Along the Old West Trails* © 1996 Teacher Ideas Press 1-800-237-6124.

over the open fire. Meat is usually tough, but the cowboys are hungry and don't complain. Pig is another good animal for meals. What isn't eaten can be well preserved for later. When we come across wild bear or deer, we see dinner on the fire. Those cowboys could hunt dear and bear for a hundred years and the hills would still be filled with 'em. Corn is a basic for our trail meals. We can eat it in mush scrapple or cooked on the cob over the fire. Good stuff. Bet you can smell the evening meal right now, wherever you might be. Cowboys do love the beef. I should mention the cowhides. We often save the skins to be used as saddle pouches for carrying things and covers for supplies. Of course, you have to treat them and scrape them and let them dry. They do smell a bit during this process.

We clean up as well as we can after each meal. We try to keep things clean so we don't end up like the dead trail crew. When we can, we have some special sweet pie for dessert—sometimes wild berries, or fruit pies when we can get the filling. Sounds great, doesn't it? Remember, never criticize the cook! Just eat and enjoy.

If you ever want to ride along and help with the cooking, you just give a holler now. You young 'uns take care, and we'll see you around the chuck wagon.

Your friend,
Alfred "Cookie" Petry

From *Galloping Along the Old West Trails*   © 1996   Teacher Ideas Press   1-800-237-6124.

Activities

The West was home to no fancy barbecue, nor were cowboys fed the king's cut of Prime Rib. If it was meat, instead of bread and beans, it was tough, charred, and red. You and your buckaroos might try some of the following Old West recipes, guaranteed to tantalize the taste buds.

Griddle Cakes

Griddle cakes, or morning cakes, are soft and aromatic like a fine, cream-colored, thin cake. Serve these with melted butter and some fine tree-drained, bucket-caught maple syrup (or a bottle of syrup from the local grocery store). Preserves work well, too.

Ingredients

$1\frac{1}{2}$ cups all-purpose white flour

$\frac{1}{2}$ cup wheat flour

$\frac{1}{2}$ teaspoon baking soda (not baking powder)

a pinch of salt

1 egg

2 cups whole milk

2 teaspoons oil

Procedure

Mix the ingredients in a large bowl, stirring until most of the lumps are gone. The batter should be thin enough to pour onto a hot greased griddle. Make the cakes about 4 inches in diameter. Cook griddle cakes over a medium flame until golden brown on one side, then flip them over and cook on the other side. Remove to a warm plate and serve.

This recipe should feed a family of four or, if overcooked, your sheepdog for three days!

Fried Mush

You'll love this one if you're ever stuck in a cave for longer than two weeks.

Ingredients

cornmeal

water

salt

Procedure

Cook cornmeal as directed on package. When thick, pour it into a loaf pan and refrigerate one hour. Cut into $\frac{1}{2}$-inch slices.

Fry the slices in $\frac{1}{4}$-inch of unsaturated oil until crispy. Serve on a plate and drizzle with pure maple syrup or honey.

Savory Stew

This savory stew has saved whole wagon trains trapped in fierce snowstorms, was served to miners when gold was discovered near the town of Murphy's California, and was once used as a lubricant in the grease horn for a stagecoach carrying a doctor traveling to perform an emergency appendectomy. So, take your pick.

Ingredients

2 pounds beef, ground or cubed

5 to 8 chopped potatoes

3 onions, chopped finely

4 carrots, sliced

1 pepper, chopped (each)

1 handful of peas

1 cup corn

pinch of pepper and salt

Procedure

In a heavy frying pan, sear beef on all sides in hot oil until brown. When the beef is almost seared, add potatoes, cut into 1-inch squares. Toss in chopped onions, carrots, green pepper, red pepper (bell pepper, not the hot stuff), peas, corn, salt, pepper and water.

Simmer for an hour. It's ready when the veggies are done but not too mushy and when the flavor is just right. Serve with warm sourdough bread.

Lone Prairie Bean Soup

This soup will feed an entire cattle drive crew and provide them the protein to put on a Wild West show!

Ingredients

a large handful of seven beans (or six will do) including white beans, small beans, lentils, black beans, kidneys, split peas, and black eyes

onions (finely chopped)

a small piece of meat: bacon, buffalo, or rattlesnake

pepper

the innards of a fiery red chili pepper (optional)

Procedure

Put the beans in a large pot, add all the other ingredients, and fill the pot three-quarters full with water. Bring to a boil, then reduce heat and simmer for three or more hours. Check the water level and add more as necessary. Check for seasoning and add whatever seems right. There are no rules.

From *Galloping Along the Old West Trails* © 1996 Teacher Ideas Press 1-800-237-6124.

Trail Mix

After a long day in the saddle, a cowpoke can become mighty hungry. This is a great all-time favorite to make with your students. Be daring and adventurous. Throw in a few gummy bears, cut-up candy bars, or healthy low-fat cereals. You're in store for a real treat and quick energy, too!

Ingredients

raisins	dried fruit
peanuts	carob chips
pretzels	dried coconut
sunflower seeds	granola cereal
chocolate chips	

Procedure

Mix one cup of three or more of the listed ingredients in a large bowl.

Butter

In the 1850s, butter was a welcome treat to spread on bread and biscuits. The time-consuming process of making it was worth it when those hot rolls came out of the oven.

Materials/Ingredients

* ★ Half a dozen medium-sized jars with screw-on lids
* ★ Bowl
* ★ Cheesecloth squares to wrap around the opening of the jars
* ★ Heavy whipping cream

Procedure

Assemble the collection of jars (those from spaghetti sauce, mayonnaise, and peanut butter work best). Make sure they are clean by running them through the dishwasher on the "hot" cycle. Pour equal amounts of heavy whipping cream into each of the jars, then tightly secure the lids.

Divide the class into half a dozen small groups. Have each group sit on the floor in a small circle. Give each group a jar and have the students take turns shaking the jar 20 times and then passing it on to the next person in the group. Be sure to point out to the students how the cream is changing, first becoming foamy and then turning into globules of butter. This is a good photo opportunity!

When the butter has fully separated from the liquid, have the students stop shaking the jars, open the lid, and pour off the liquid into a large bowl. What remains is honest-to-goodness, homemade butter. There's just one problem: it's bitter. To get rid of the bitter taste, wash the butter in water. You might also add a little salt, kneading it in. Serve it to the students on crackers, bread, or hot biscuits.

The Cowboy and the Black-Eyed Pea

Have you ever looked at that little pea with the black spot on one side? You wonder why the Almighty made such a little critter of a bean. It's as though a lima bean got shrunk down so small that it got lost from all the other little beans on the way west. It just laid out on the plains for years bleaching by day and darkening by night. One day the moon passed between the sun and the earth blocking out the light of the day and sending a moon shadow down on that little pea, making a dark spot where the moon light would never shine again. The black-eyed pea was born! You can believe it or not, but during the next solar eclipse, quietly look inside your cupboard and see what all those tiny black-eyed peas are doing. You might be very surprised.

The meals of the cowboy could hardly be called nutritious. Prepared by the trail cook on the chuck wagon, the food was dull and generally unhealthy. The cowboy's diet consisted mostly of coffee, sugar, dried fruit flour, rice, and beans. Black-eyed peas occasionally found their way onto the dinner tin as well.

Objective

Students will use the black-eyed pea to practice and reinforce estimation skills.

Materials

* ✶ Black-eyed peas (enough to give each student a small handful)
* ✶ Glue
* ✶ A copy of the book *The Cowboy and the Black-Eyed Pea,* by Tony Johnston and Warren Ludwig
* ✶ *The Cowboy and the Black-Eyed Pea* activity sheet (see page 62)

Procedure

Read aloud with "gusto and verve" the Western fairy tale *The Cowboy and the Black-Eyed Pea* by Tony Johnston and Warren Ludwig. Because this integrated math activity involves using black-eyed peas to determine the area and perimeter of selected shapes, you will need to explain the mathematical terms *estimation, area,* and *perimeter.* Demonstrate on the chalkboard what each term means.

Distribute a small handful of black-eyed peas to each student. Following the directions on the activity sheet provided on the next page, have the students estimate, calculate, and solve the mathematical problems.

From *Galloping Along the Old West Trails* © 1996 Teacher Ideas Press 1-800-237-6124.

The Cowboy and the Black-Eyed Pea

Name _____

1. Estimate the number of black-eyed peas in your bag or cup. Record the number. Count the beans. Determine the difference between the two numbers.

    Estimated number in bag   _____

    Actual number count   _____

    Difference   _____

2. Estimate the number of black-eyed peas needed to measure the perimeter and the area of the horseshoe shape (see fig. 11.1).

    Perimeter estimation   _____

    Area estimation   _____

3. Glue the black-eyed peas around the perimeter of the horseshoe. How many are needed?

    Perimeter   _____

4. Glue more black-eyed peas to fill in the horseshoe. Record the number needed to fill in the horseshoe.

    Area   _____

5. Find the difference between your estimates and the actual numbers.

    Estimates   _____

    Actual   _____

From *Galloping Along the Old West Trails* © 1996 Teacher Ideas Press 1-800-237-6124.

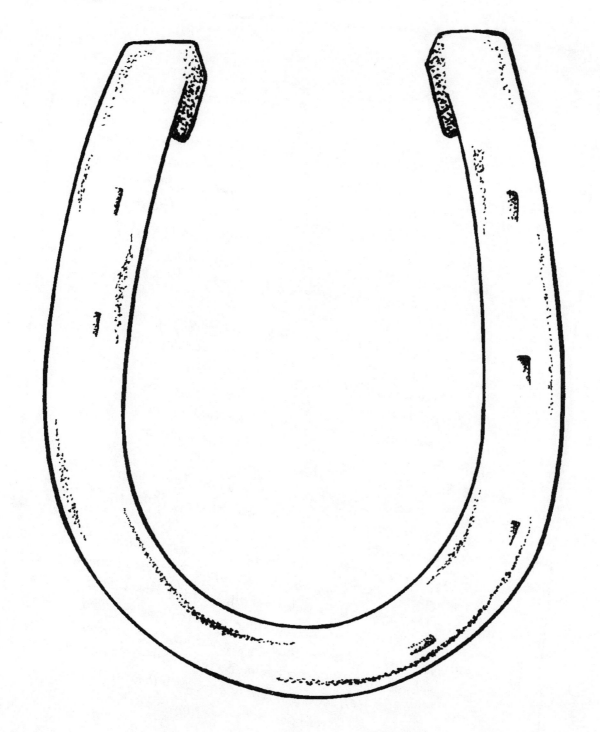

Figure 11.1 The horseshoe for estimating the number of black-eyed peas

Letter 12
A Small Town in Sight

With still more days behind us, and dust and cold a way of life, we approach what we think is a small town out in the distance. When we bedded down last night, all we could see was a small flickering of light many miles down the trail. If that is a town up ahead, we're hoping to stop and refresh, get some home cooking (without dust), take a bath, and get inside. We'll know if there really is a town when the sun comes up.

It's now about 10 in the morning. Don't wear a pocket watch as they only get full of dirt and stop working on a trail ride like we're on. We learn to tell the time by the height of the sun in the sky. We know that if it is almost winter, the sun will be to the south and it will not rise straight above us at noon like it would in the summer months. So, at 10, it is just about even with my shoulder, and at noon it is about straight out from my ear. Try it some time and get a feeling for the tools of the trail. Don't need no fancy gold watch out here.

As we were just stopping the herd for lunch (our lunch and the cattle's lunch), we could see a little dust cloud rising from the trail some three miles off toward the town. Soon we could see that it was a lone rider coming right toward us. All eyes were following that figure until before us was a man wearing a silver star on his vest. He introduced himself as the town sheriff. He was friendly enough, but he did have a serious message. He told us that each time a cattle drive

A Small Town in Sight

From *Galloping Along the Old West Trails* © 1996 Teacher Ideas Press 1-800-237-6124.

comes to his town, he always comes out to meet it and share the rules. For this drive, it was no different. He welcomed us to town but said that he wanted no trouble, and if we were to come into "his" town, he would expect that all guns would be turned in at the sheriff's office until such time as we were leaving. He also said that there would be no fights, no breaking of furniture, and no bothering the local townsfolk. The trail boss assured him that we were here to drive the cattle through town, and we were not going to cause any problems. I liked the sheriff and his straightforward approach to the situation. I had never met a small town western sheriff, so I hoped I would have an opportunity to talk with him when I was in town. Maybe he will also talk to you about the law of the West. We shall see.

We will be stopping at a cattle ranch in a day or two before heading back on the Chisholm Trail. Will write to you then. Hope you're keeping track of where we are. If anyone from back at Quincy comes looking for me, you'll be able to tell them where we are. One more day, one more sunset.

Your friends,
The Cowboy, Kaper King,
and Sierra

Letter from the
Town Sheriff

Sheriff Langton is what they call me. I've been the sheriff here for two years now. You probably hear that the only time a sheriff gets the job is when the previous sheriff gets killed by some notorious outlaw. Not the case here. The previous sheriff, Mr. Cartland, met a fine young lady passing through from Boston and fell in love with her. He quit his job, and the two of them joined a wagon train to Utah. So here I am, as I said two years, trying to uphold and enforce the law of this town.

I've had some fierce times with outlaws, card sharks, and horse thieves. But most of the time, it isn't real exciting. I deal with cowboys who have had too much to drink or a couple of ranchers who are feuding over unbranded cattle. I sit some of the hotheads in the jail overnight and take their weapons until they are on the outskirts of town. When a cattle drive is coming through town, I usually ride out and meet it and let everyone know the rules before they cross the town boundary. If I sense any trouble coming, I have time to call my deputies (who are 20 of the townsfolk who have other jobs) and we set up a barricade at the entrance to the main street and let the troublemakers know they can just keep moving to the next town. Usually, they just do it, as they don't want to jeopardize the herd. A trail boss who causes harm to a herd will either never get a job with a ranch again or will simply be shot. So, they avoid trouble when they can, and the peace is preserved. We have had a couple of shoot-outs in town, and fortunately I've either been faster on the draw or my deputies helped out. Normally, this is quite a peaceful place. I like it that way, and so do the townsfolk. Sure, I wear a gun, like most lawmen, but I wear it so I don't have to use it.

Today the sun is shining, and I think I have time to plant some flowers in those boxes in front of my office. They'll spruce up the place a bit. You stay safe, and if you come to town, stop by my office. I'll show you around.

Sheriff Langton

Letter from the Town Sheriff

From *Galloping Along the Old West Trails* © 1996   Teacher Ideas Press   1-800-237-6124.

Activities

Law in the West was clear-cut and to the point. If you broke the law and were caught, you were tossed in the hoosegow. Many an infamous outlaw spent time in the local jail (and a few were hung from the closest tree).

The Moral

Present your students with everyday issues that require decision making based on moral judgment. Pose the following scenarios to the class. Ask them to make a journal entry responding to the circumstances. Let them think about the action they might take and the possible consequences.

1. Suppose you find a gold chain on the floor. It is bright and shiny and you have always wanted one. What would you do?

2. Your best friend asks you to help him or her cheat on a test. What would you do?

3. You failed a test and have to have it signed by your parent. You will lose a recess if it is not returned. Would you forge the signature?

4. You discover a beautiful white, 16-hand horse grazing by the river. No one is around. If you take the horse and are caught as a horse thief, you will be hung from the nearest tree. If you leave the horse, it may become injured, get lost, or die. What would you do?

Wanted Posters

As your students learn about law and order in an old western town, have them create wanted posters for the outlaws of the day. Such bandits as Jesse James, Billy the Kid, and Belle Star terrorized the territories and became legends. Have students research the characters, then create posters listing their crimes. (For a sample poster, see page 69.)

U.S. TERRITORY
Information & Reward

$100.00 REWARD IN GOLD COIN

For Anyone Providing Information Regarding the Untimely Death of the U.S. Marshall in the Nebraska Territories

On November 22, 1857, U.S. Marshall Scoleri was found dead from unknown causes. The body of the Marshall was discovered at the base of a large tree on the open plains. His horse has never been found. His colt revolver was still in his side holster and no personal possessions were missing. Honey was discovered near the tree. His body was discovered by a young pioneer family heading west. They surmised that the death had occurred some three days before they happened by. The family returned the Marshall's body to the near- est town and has voluntarily delayed their journey west awaiting next of kin to arrive from Abeline.

If you can provide any information please contact the nearest
U.S. Marshall office or local Sheriff.

If you are interested in applying for the job of Marshall send telegraph wire to U.S. Marshall-Western Territories.

Rewards are paid within six months of verification of information.

Activities   69

The Silver Badge

The lawmen of the West wore a badge representing law and justice. Deputize your students for the day. Give them a shiny silver star to wear (made out of aluminum foil). Have them search out random acts of kindness on the playground and in the hallways. Award "the good deed doers" with a silver star to wear, too! As an extension activity, students can design and make the deputy badge of choice.

Letter 13
Down South in Texas

We have arrived near the end of the Shawnee Trail, and after a brief stop at a large cattle ranch, we will be heading north again up the Chisholm Trail. So far, the drive has gone well. I've learned a great deal about cattle driving. The cattle are in pretty good shape, and the crew has remained intact, except for one fella who stepped in a rock pile and got himself a nasty broken ankle. Fortunately, we were still near that last town and were able to send for help. The town doctor (or was he a dentist?) came out in his buckboard wagon and took the guy back to his office. He'll probably have to stay there for a week or two, and then they will put him back on a stage going to Kansas. A bad piece of luck for that fella. He had told us that he was trying to earn enough money on the cattle drive to send for his family when he finally made it West. Guess that won't be happening any time soon. It makes you feel you are lucky that nothing has gone wrong. We'll just keep our fingers crossed and watch where we step.

It rained again last night, and the rivers are becoming unpredictable. Hope Mother Nature holds out until we begin our trip north. Glad I have those red long johns and an extra saddle blanket to keep me warm. I wear a poncho that actually comes down over my saddle to keep the rain off me and my gear. My hat keeps both the sun, when it's shining, and the rain out of my face.

Anyway, we are approaching our last stop south, sometime tomorrow. That should put us near the big cattle ranch that has been our destination. I'll write again very soon.

Sincerely,
The Cowboy, Kaper King,
and Sierra

Letter from the
Cattle Rancher

Name's Kelly James. I am the owner of the Lost River Ranch down here in Texas. I'm waiting for the herd of cattle coming down the Shawnee Trail to be dropped off here on the ranch. The same crew will round up and take back a fattened herd of longhorns that will go to the trains and then to the stockyards and back East for the beef markets. The longhorn originally came across the Atlantic Ocean from Spain. Of course these didn't come from Spain, couldn't swim that far ... just a joke. Actually they were driven up from Mexico. Might add that this area was part of Mexico a few years back.

My ranch is 6,000 acres of prime grazing land, and I have cattle scattered everywhere. The range is not fully fenced as that would require too great an expense, and it just isn't necessary. We ranchers down here brand our cattle with the sign of our ranch. The cattle sometimes just mix together, but at sorting time we take ours and leave the ones that belong to our neighbors. There was a time when only a few ranchers were branding, and outsiders would come in and place their brand on our cattle. Never could understand dishonest folks. If we caught rustlers taking our cattle or horses, they were quickly hung from the nearest tree. That is range justice and it is no secret. You never mess with a man's herd, and you never take his horse. The message spread quickly and rustlers learned this was not a place to operate.

If you don't take good care of your cattle on the drive, they can lose too much weight, which is bad news. Every pound lost is money out of my pocket. So, the drivers need to let them eat along the way and keep them healthy. Our other fear is disease. "Black leg" or tuberculosis can decimate the entire herd. If the rancher suspects there are any diseased cattle, we must separate the sick animals and destroy them immediately. If a rancher tries to save his sick cattle, they can infect the cattle throughout the territory and ruin the entire stock for years. One year a small rancher who knew his cattle were sick nevertheless tried to run them to market. When the neighboring ranchers learned of this, we all had to go to our friend and convince him to destroy his herd. He refused. So we had to take the law into our own hands for the sake of all the ranchers. We were forced to shoot all 200 of his cattle. He just didn't understand. Once his ranch was cleaned, we all loaned him cattle to start a new herd. That was four years ago, and today his herd is healthy and strong again.

Ranching is hard work. Most cowboys are up before the sun and to bed just after sundown. We have our fun too, but mostly it's just hard work. We'll be watching for the northern trail crew coming south. It's always interesting with new cowboys and fresh cattle. Perhaps some of you will be coming our way and will take on some work at the ranch. Ask any of the cowboys on the Shawnee or Chisholm Trails, and they will direct you to the Lost River.

I think I see a cloud of dust in the distance. It's either a blowing storm or the drive coming home. Good-bye now.

Sincerely,
Kelly James

From *Galloping Along the Old West Trails* © 1996 Teacher Ideas Press 1-800-237-6124.

Activities

Every child has dreamed of roping, riding, and branding out on the western ranch. With our Cowboy and Rancher, students in your class can participate in the life of a cowboy/cowgirl.

Visit a Local Ranch

Just look out there a yonder (or open the yellow pages) and you will no doubt find a fine ranch for your class to visit. Be sure it is a cattle ranch. (No ostrich breeding ranches!) And, don't forget your boots and brown bag lunch.

For city folks who can't get to a ranch, a videocassette is available: *Cowboys on the Job.* Contact On the Job Productions, PO Box 3421, Quartz Hill, CA 93586-0421. The tape is approximately 30 minutes long.

Join the Cattle Drive

Have students solve the following problem:

You are driving a herd of 300 cattle up the Shawnee Trail to a railroad yard. Each steer weighed 800 pounds at the start of the drive. After a week the herd lost a total of 4,000 pounds. The trail boss decided to graze the cattle for a week, and each steer gained 10 pounds. The cattle drive continued to the rail line, and upon arrival, all cattle were weighed in. Each steer had lost 5 more pounds. The cattle buyer paid 20 cents a pound. How much was the rancher paid in total for the steers?

A Western Bar-B-Q

It doesn't really matter what you're studying as long as food is involved. Big and little buckaroos alike will enjoy the fun of a western Bar-B-Q. Use beef for the burgers (not tofu or turkey). Fire up those coals (or the gas stove) and get ready to cook the best tasting burgers on Earth. Have a variety of condiments on hand (although kids still sing those sweet words, "I'll take mine plain!"). Accompany those burgers with authentic molasses, oven-baked beans—straight from the supermarket! You can soak pintos and make authentic refried beans, if you want, and corn on the cob and a root beer will make your Western outdoor feast complete.

Branding

Cattle roamed the wide open ranges in the early days of the American cowboy. Because the animals would often band together (no matter to whom they belonged), branding became the most practical way to identify ownership. Each ranch would have its own simple mark, which would be sizzled into the hide of the animal with a fire-heated branding iron. Later, when the roundup took place, the cattle owners could identify their cattle easily.

Objective

Students will design an original branding mark.

Materials

* ★ Brown construction paper
* ★ Brown paint
* ★ Pipe cleaners

Procedure

Give each student a pipe cleaner. Instruct them to create a simple design by bending their pipe cleaner into a unique shape. The design could represent their initials, a geometric shape, or an Indian pictograph. The branding tool must be flat and the simple construction of a short handle for gripping is useful. Make a short handle by twisting another pipe cleaner and attaching it tot he brand. This will prevent little fingers from getting dirty.

Give each student a piece of brown construction paper and have them carefully crumble it. Continue the crumbling until the construction paper takes on the look of real leather, then gently smooth the paper flat.

Dip the pipe cleaner "branding iron" into a dollop of brown paint. Be sure that the flat surface of the brand is completely covered with paint. Brand the "leather" with the pipe cleaner by pressing it firmly onto the paper's surface. Depending on the skill and age of your group, you may want to practice branding on scratch paper before using the "leather."

When dry, display these branding marks on a bulletin board. They will be proud symbols of ownership.

From *Galloping Along the Old West Trails* © 1996 Teacher Ideas Press 1-800-237-6124.

Letter 14
A Big Surprise

I don't know how much mail you are getting, and for all I know, you may be writing to some other cowboy riding on the southern trail through the Arizona territories. I'm beginning to think of all of you guys as my family. The weather is good, the ground is a bit soggy, and the new cattle are eager, excited, and probably a little scared as we prepare to head north.

Before we left San Antonio and the ranch, a few of the men left the trail crew to do other things, and some new folks signed on. That seems to be the way it goes on the cattle drive. Tonight we were all just relaxing, talking and sitting around a large fire in the courtyard of the ranch in front of the main bunkhouse. That's where the hired help stay while working. The family who owns the ranch has a real nice house off to the side across the creek. The sound of the creek is calming as the water skips over the rocks day and night. Anyway, it was getting late and it was time to call it a night. We all needed to get some sleep so we would be ready for the first day of the ride north. Several of the crew got up, and we headed for the bunkhouse.

I noticed this one cowboy heading off to the side of the bunkhouse. I said, "This is the way over here." He looked up at me, and in a voice that I had never heard before said, "Goodnight, Cowboy. I'm sleeping in the barn." The cowboy took off his hat, and shiny long black hair fell

A Big Surprise

From *Galloping Along the Old West Trails* © 1996 Teacher Ideas Press 1-800-237-6124.

onto his shoulders. It was a woman! I looked twice and said, "Excuse me, ma'am, I didn't know you were a woman." She said, "I know. I always want it that way for the first day or two on the trail. Savannah is my name, Savannah Rain." "Well, goodnight, Miss Rain," I said, removing my hat. "Goodnight, Cowboy," she said with a lovely smile. "Call me Savannah. See you in the morning."

I didn't sleep well at all that night. I had never before met a cowgirl. Hmm … Savannah.

The Cowboy

Letter from a Cowgirl

Most people think of the cowboys as the men who tamed the West, driving cattle, settling the territories, and exploring the prairie. For the most part that is true, or at least that is what you always hear described. Yet, many women like me had a role in the shaping of the frontier. Of course, women were in the same places as men. Sometimes the cowgirls were as strong and talented as the cowboys. Understand that men never liked women doing their work, so many women had to disguise themselves just to get the job. It didn't happen too often, but it happened to me.

After Ma died of the fever, Pa, who still had a ranch up north, taught me how to ride.

I felt the need to head West, so I took a job on a cattle drive, but only after I disguised myself as a man. I rode into a trail camp on a Shawnee Trail ranch and stood in line with the other cowboys. My clothes were worn and baggy, my boots were dirty, and I was wearing a hat just like the other cowboys. I had a large neckerchief around my neck and a lot of dirt on my face. I walked up to the table near the ranch house and said, "Looking for work with the herd." The ranch boss looked at me and said, "Kind of short. Can you rope?" I assured him I could and told him I had worked on the crews from here to Missouri. He stared at me again, and before he

Letter from a Cowgirl

From *Galloping Along the Old West Trails* © 1996 Teacher Ideas Press 1-800-237-6124.

could say anything else, I grabbed the rope hanging on the hitching rail and roped three cowboys walking toward the bunkhouse. "You're hired!" he said. I touched my hat and said, "Rain is my name." He wrote it down and directed me to the bunkhouse, but I had to stay in the stable area for obvious reasons.

Tonight, while leaving the campfire, I met a nice cowboy. He is the one riding that fine horse. I said goodnight to him, but we both knew that we would like to get to know each other better. Sometimes it gets really lonely out here, and I imagine what life would be like if I was to settle down. Neither a woman nor a man can spend an entire life out here on the range. This seems to be the world for rough and tough. Tonight I'm not feeling so rough, and maybe the truth is I'm feeling soft. Well, thinking about it, a woman like me can do both if I want. I know I'm good at what I do, and I do like being a woman. Still though, I would like to spend a bit more time with that traveling cowboy. He did seem quite different from the rest. We shall see.

We're on the trail again tomorrow, and I have to be at my best just like any of the men. This still is an exciting life. I do love it.

I wish you all a good night. My best to you.

Your new friend,
Savannah Rain

Letter from a Cowgirl

79

Activity

In today's society, where women compete equally with men in many walks of life, it is difficult to imagine the awe created by rodeo great Annie Oakley. She embarked on a quest few women pursued in the era of perceived male supremacy. Her theatrical sharpshooting gained her the name "Little Sure Shot." She competed with the best as she toured with the Buffalo Bill Wild West Show and gained legendary status that lives on today.

Women of the Wild West

Challenge your students to collect and research information on the lives of famous women from the western era. Have them read diaries, journals, and letters by women who lived during the expansion of this country and who recorded their perspective of the time they lived. These women may include:

★ Dame Shirley (Mrs. Fayette Clappe), who wrote about life in California during the Gold Rush

★ Laura Ingalls Wilder, author of several books about life on the prairie

★ Lotta Crabtree and Lola Montez, entertainers in California during the Gold Rush

★ Cynthia Ann Parker, white captive of the Comanche Indians and mother of the famed chief Quanah Parker

Create a bulletin board featuring abstract art portraits of the women. Use the art of tearing. Show the students how to control the tearing by using the thumb of the left hand to hold the paper down and the right hand to pull away small pieces of paper. Use torn paper for every part of the portrait: eyes, nose, lips, hair, jewelry, hats, etc. Indicate to the students that an item symbolizing each woman should be pasted to the lower right section of the face. For instance, Annie Oakley would have her rifles and Laura Ingalls would have a covered wagon.

Letter 15
My Fine Horse Threw a Shoe

We're still heading north on the Chisholm Trail, and it seems to get colder with each day closer to winter. Texas offers different vistas as we pass from town to town. Some of the towns are so small they almost seem like a speck as we quickly pass through. Others have more life, and you can tell that these will someday be real nice cities. You just watch the people doing what they do and you know what is going to happen. If you see women working and children running and playing, you know this will be a growing town. You just can feel the pride of the townspeople knowing they are building something real special for tomorrow. Maybe I'll find myself a nice town like some of these when I get to the Pacific coast. I'd like a place with good stores and fine, well-kept houses. I'd like to know that the kids are getting an education and attending a good school. Should be a church in town, too. Maybe that's in my future.

Today, I was riding one of the extra horses on the drive, as Kaper King lost his right rear shoe. Sometimes in deep sand or when a horse trips over its own feet, the metal shoe will pull loose and tear away, taking a small chunk of the hoof with it. That's what happened this morning. We stepped in some gooey mud just on the other side of this small river. It was like quicksand and just sucked that shoe right off Kaper King's back foot. Took a little bit of hoof with it. It doesn't hurt the horse, because horses don't have nerves in the hoof. But it could hurt if a puncture went real deep into the foot. The material the hoof is made from is quite similar to the material our fingernails are

My Fine Horse Threw a Shoe

From *Galloping Along the Old West Trails* © 1996 Teacher Ideas Press 1-800-237-6124.

made from. Anyway, it sure looks nasty! And, of course, without a shoe, he would be more apt to get a stone bruise if I was riding him.

So, today Kaper King is tied to one of the wagons and is just "going along for the ride." Did you ever wonder where that old saying came from? He doesn't seem to mind, just trottin' along behind the wagon. In fact, I think he's quite enjoying himself. That stinker! The horse I'm riding just doesn't have that smooth walk and trot that Kaper King has. Every horse rides a bit differently.

It might be interesting for you to see one of those medical charts showing the physiology of a horse. You might have some books that would show the parts of a horse, especially the legs and feet.

Tomorrow, we will be in the next town, and I'm hoping that I can find a farrier who can fit Kaper King with a new shoe. We rely more and more on people with a variety of skills different from our own. It would be difficult for me to shape a hot piece of metal into a horseshoe, but then again, it may be hard for a farrier to drive cattle. Interesting thought. Until we write again.

Your friends,
The Cowboy, Kaper King
(on three feet), and Sierra

My Fine Horse Threw a Shoe

Letter from the Farrier

I've been kicked 10 feet up against the wooden sides of the barn. I've had my hand burned so that I couldn't move my fingers for three weeks, and my back aches from bending over so that I often feel like a twisted old man at the ripe old age of 30. But darn, I love what I do. I'm the town farrier. I'm my own boss! I can sing or talk or just listen to the sound of my hammer hitting the hot metal against the heavy anvil. I can listen to the horses and hear the stories of their adventures. I know many a famous outlaw, not because they ever talked to me, but because I gave their horses kind treatment and healthy hooves. Yep, no lawman, messenger, cowboy, or outlaw could get by without a good farrier.

In case you don't know it, I take care of the feet of most of the horses in this town. Those that belong to the regular townspeople and those of the folks just passing through. Most people, especially city people, don't know that horses' hooves grow just like our fingernails. If you don't properly trim 'em and file 'em, the feet will get sore and disfigured, and the horse will become crippled and hardly able to move. So nearly every six to eight weeks, I will pull the old shoes from the horses and either make new ones or refit the old ones. First I need to chip down the hoof with a very sharp knife, gently carving it like a fine piece of Eastern cherry wood, cut it, level, and smooth it, getting it ready for the metal shoe. The heated metal is formed into a U-shaped shoe in a hot coal oven. It is checked, cooled, rechecked,

---

heated, and cooled again until it fits just so. The new shoe is then nailed into the hoof with the nails being cut off along the sides. I do this again on the other three feet, taking a total of about an hour and a half. It's hot, backbreaking work, but that's what I do. So, if you are walking down the street of our town and you hear the ringing of the hammer hitting the shoe on the anvil, you'll know that the farrier is hard at work.

Some folks say it is the sheriff or the railroad that is winning the West. I know it is the majestic horse and his friend the farrier.

Take care of your horses,
Jack, the Farrier

Activity

The Cowboy spent a day in town having his horse shoed by the local farrier. With all those shoes lying all over the place, the teacher down the road in that one-room schoolhouse ought to be able to use them for some interesting art. Here goes!

Do Horseshoes Look Back?

Objective

The students will construct an authentic horseshoe photo art project.

Materials

* ★ Authentic horseshoes
* ★ Camera, film
* ★ Bandanna
* ★ Cowboy hat or other Western attire
* ★ Black nontoxic spray paint
* ★ Bucket
* ★ Wire brush
* ★ Scissors
* ★ Glue sticks or liquid glue, and a glue gun
* ★ Tagboard

You will need real horseshoes. New ones can be purchased from a horseshoe supply store or western outfitter store. Your best bet is to visit a local stable and bring along a big plastic bucket with a heavy-duty handle. Ask the proprietor (or farrier if he or she is there) to save the old horseshoes the next time shoeing comes around. For your information, horses need shoeing about every six weeks (in 1860 it was only two bits or so, but today it's $50 to $100). You'll need at least one horseshoe per student and one for yourself to make a prototype. (Or, you can use the template in fig. 15.2.)

Procedure

Photograph each child in western attire, using a bandanna, a cowboy hat, and any other western accessories you can amass. Once you've taken the pictures and had them developed, you will need to demonstrate the procedure. Do this *before* you pass out the materials.

Lay out all the materials we've mentioned before you begin. Clean the horseshoes with a wire brush. Take the shoes outside and lay them on newspaper, then spray them with the black paint. (You may want to do these two steps yourself ahead of time and relieve the kids of getting scratched and covered with paint. If you should decide on this approach, begin instead with the next step.)

Lay the horseshoe ends up (for good luck, of course) over the picture, framing the best parts of the photo. With a pencil or pen trace a line around the outside of the shoe on the picture. Remove the shoe and set it aside. Do the same with the tagboard.

Activity

With scissors, cut along the line. Your photo will have the shape of the outer edge of the horseshoe. Set the photo aside and do the same with the tagboard. The photo and tagboard should be the same shape and size.

Using a glue stick or liquid glue, attach the photo, face up, to the tagboard. (See fig. 15.1.)

Apply the glue to the edges of the shoe and the photo with the tagboard backing. The students can press the pieces together tightly for a minute or two until the glue sets. When everything is set and cool, they can trim any remaining photo, tagboard, or glue, then hang their works of art in a giant horseshoe pattern for all to see.

FIGURE 15.1 SAMPLE HORSESHOE PHOTO PROJECT

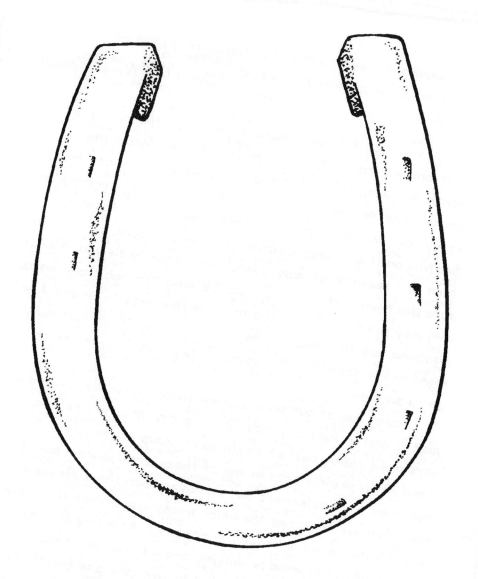

FIGURE 15.2 KAPER KING'S HORSESHOE

the curtain of flame was only a few yards deep and that we would emerge on scorched but flameless soil on the other side. It would catch us regardless, so we thought it would be better to run through it than be caught still.

For the next few minutes we all used what water we had in the store wagons to wet our clothing, especially our bandannas, which were now covering our faces. I heard that the heat and smoke could be so intense that they would singe your lungs and kill you on the spot if you breathed too deeply. I pulled open my saddlebags and took out two of my extra shirts and ripped off the sleeves. I soaked them in water and pulled each onto Kaper King's legs, first the front, and then the back. They were like big wet socks that hopefully would protect his legs from the fire. I tied his tail back and poured the remaining water over his face. I grabbed Sierra and put her in the first passing wagon. She looked at me and wagged her tail. I yelled, "You stay there, girl!"

We were going through it! The trail boss gave the call, and all the cattle crew whistled and yelled. We drove the cattle right into the burning sage. The snorting, neighing, yelling, and whistling were deafening as we entered the blackness of the burning prairie. The heat was intense and the smoke all but choked what energy we had left. But within seconds, we emerged on the other side, where the charred earth was quietly still smoking.

We quickly pulled down our bandannas from our faces and yelled and hollered. We were just happy we were alive. One wagon was on fire, but we quickly threw dirt on the flames and watched as the final sparks quivered and

A Day I Will Never Forget

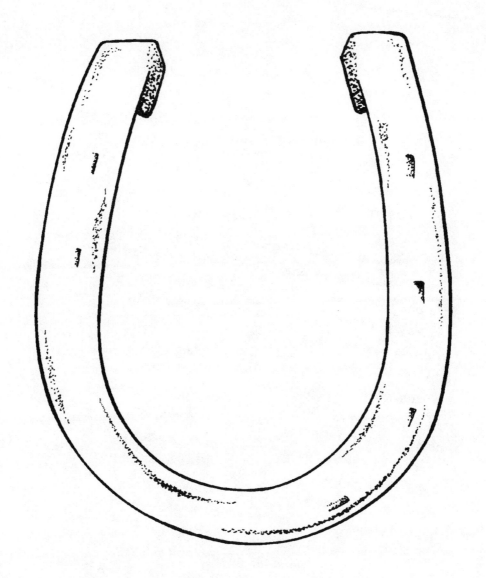

Figure 15.2 Kaper King's Horseshoe

Letter 16
A Day I Will Never Forget

It won't be too many more days before the cattle drive is over and we leave the Chisholm Trail behind. We continue north, and with the end of the ride comes real money in my pocket. I better watch where I put it because I now have holes in my vest and pants pockets. Your clothing sure takes a beating on these rides. Learned to sew and darn, as you can't turn to a seamstress, lady friend, or mother to fix your things. I sure don't want that cool breeze blowing through those holes. Anyway, partners, when the trail north comes to an end, I will again be heading west on the famous Oregon Trail, hopefully right to the great Pacific Ocean. I sure look forward to that day. I sure do.

Today, one of our scouts came galloping wildly toward us just as fast as he could ride. "Prairie fire, prairie fire!" he screamed, riding past us to the next group of the crew. I've read about prairie fires in one of those small journal books published for Easterners, but I'd never seen them. As we all looked up, we could see the black smoke low across the horizon, just where we were headed. It doesn't take a fire long to spread when the wind is blowing and where, even though it is almost winter, the scrub brush is brown, dry, and brittle. I once heard it said that a prairie fire can overtake a trail crew in minutes. If you panic or don't know what you're doing, all the cattle and wagons can burn before you realize what has happened.

From *Galloping Along the Old West Trails* © 1996 Teacher Ideas Press 1-800-237-6124.

The trail boss called us together. Everyone looked genuinely concerned, in fact downright scared. I know I was. We had reason to be. Haven't ever been through anything like this. No one knows how these fires get started. Could be a careless trail crew who didn't put out their fires, outlaws trying to block the path of a pursuing posse, a careless campfire, or even a lightning storm. Didn't really matter, because it came nearer.

The cattle were all getting very nervous, and they began to move together and snort. The smoke was getting darker and was beginning to block out the sun like a giant curtain draped along the sky. It became completely black up ahead, in contrast to the south, which was still just as blue as blue can be. A mighty strange sight indeed. Kaper King raised his head toward the fire and his nostrils flared. My sweet dog, Sierra, had been following behind but now was right by our side as we planned our advance.

The scout and trail boss said that the fire seemed to have a front miles wide and was advancing very quickly, creating its own wind from the heat that it generated. We would not have the time to turn around and go back or to go around the fire. Fortunately, the brush was low and the fire was only a few feet in height. Still hot, dangerous, and a potential killer, it looked as if it would be upon us in only a few minutes.

As we tried to keep the cattle calm, we could see the orange flames eating up acre after acre of brushland as it moved toward us. It was decided that we would drive the cattle and wagons right through the fire, hoping that

---

A Day I Will Never Forget

From *Galloping Along the Old West Trails* © 1996   Teacher Ideas Press   1-800-237-6124.

the curtain of flame was only a few yards deep and that we would emerge on scorched but flameless soil on the other side. It would catch us regardless, so we thought it would be better to run through it than be caught still.

For the next few minutes we all used what water we had in the store wagons to wet our clothing, especially our bandannas, which were now covering our faces. I heard that the heat and smoke could be so intense that they would singe your lungs and kill you on the spot if you breathed too deeply. I pulled open my saddlebags and took out two of my extra shirts and ripped off the sleeves. I soaked them in water and pulled each onto Kaper King's legs, first the front, and then the back. They were like big wet socks that hopefully would protect his legs from the fire. I tied his tail back and poured the remaining water over his face. I grabbed Sierra and put her in the first passing wagon. She looked at me and wagged her tail. I yelled, "You stay there, girl!"

We were going through it! The trail boss gave the call, and all the cattle crew whistled and yelled. We drove the cattle right into the burning sage. The snorting, neighing, yelling, and whistling were deafening as we entered the blackness of the burning prairie. The heat was intense and the smoke all but choked what energy we had left. But within seconds, we emerged on the other side, where the charred earth was quietly still smoking. We quickly pulled down our bandannas from our faces and yelled and hollered. We were just happy we were alive. One wagon was on fire, but we quickly threw dirt on the flames and watched as the final sparks quivered and

_____

90   **A Day I Will Never Forget**

From *Galloping Along the Old West Trails* © 1996 Teacher Ideas Press 1-800-237-6124.

died. Four cattle ran off and may have been overcome by the smoke. A few horses and most of the cattle did get some burns on their legs, mostly just a little singed hair. Most would recover within a few days. One of the crew fell to the fiery ground when his horse panicked and bolted. He received some burns to the hands and legs, but would be OK. He would be under a doctor's care at the next town.

I guess we will never know how the fire started or when it extinguished itself. All we know is that we made it safely through and that the cattle drive would soon be entering its last leg. I will never forget this day! I'll write again soon.

Your friends,
The Cowboy, Kaper King,
and Sierra

From *Galloping Along the Old West Trails*   © 1996   Teacher Ideas Press   1-800-237-6124.

Letter 17
Leaving Friends from the
Cattle Drive

We are almost to the end of the cattle drive, and tonight we entered our last town. Most of the cattle will be sold. Some will be sold for meat. Others will be raised and nourished to make up a new herd for next year. We met some wonderful people on this run, and some will be friends who will remain in my memory for a lifetime.

As we entered the fine little town, we couldn't help but notice painted banners and signs all around the main street. These banners were trying to persuade the people of the town to vote for one of the two candidates who wanted to be the new town mayor. Don't know much about the local politics, but if you want to find out, visit one of the public gathering spots like the saloon, hotel, restaurant, or even the bathhouse.

A few of the trail crew went to the hotel for dinner, where we were greeted with much exciting talk of the upcoming election. Seems that folks here are talking about whether men should own other people and keep slaves. It's been a tradition for years, mainly in the South, but many of the states don't think this is the way our country should be. It is a new way of thinking for many. Seems to me that all people are basically the same. Sure, some are small and some are tall and some have habits I don't like. I'm sure some people don't like me either, but we're all people. But, traditions are hard things to move away from. According to what I hear, this is going to be a very important election and may shape the ways to come. If I get more information or meet the candidates, I'll try to have them write.

I'm getting very excited, not only because of the election in town but also because I will soon be on my way west again. Hope all of you are well and growing strong. You all take care now, and I'll write soon.

The Cowboy, Kaper
King, and Sierra
(She's here someplace!)

Letter from a Politician for New Ideas

Hello there, my constituents! Yes, you. The constituents are those citizens who live within the territory who can vote in the upcoming election. On occasion some have been known to cast a vote even if they didn't live in the area! So any free man can vote for the next mayor of this town.

I'm glad you have come to this fine flourishing little town on your way west. Perhaps it would be worth your time to stop and consider this a good place to make your home. Perhaps this here is the sparkling end of the rainbow that you have been searching for; perhaps fate has brought you here. And not a better time either, as soon we will have an election to determine the quality of life in our wonderful town.

As long as you are here, let me tell you briefly what will happen if you cast your vote for me, Melvin McClarin, and I become the next mayor of our town. First, I will see that this becomes a town of pride. We want our town to be a good place to raise our children. So, with my election we are going to advertise in the "Boston Journal" and bring to our town two more teachers for our school. I will bring before the council the resolution to pay all travel expenses of these fine teachers, pay them $4 a month and, if single, provide a place for them to live for a modest fee or light work.

Second, we want this town to be safe from outlaws and vagabonds. I will give the sheriff a part-time deputy and immediately authorize the construction of two new jail cells adjacent to our current jailhouse.

From *Galloping Along the Old West Trails* © 1996 Teacher Ideas Press 1-800-237-6124.

Next, we need to consider very carefully whether it is desirable for the railroad to maintain a stop in our town. Of course, the railroad has a few small drawbacks, but this is the 1850s, and the railroad is the unstoppable symbol of this nation's growth, progress, and prosperity. With the railroad comes business, money, new services, and all the products from the East that we have been dreaming of for so long. The railroad companies are investing heavily in this country, and those towns that put out the welcome mat will be the beneficiaries of this investment. We stand to become a rich town as we become part of the silver ribbon of track that stretches from coast to coast. You be on the train that votes for Melvin, and you'll be on the train of progress.

Finally, we have been asked again and again to take a stand on this issue called "Abolition." This may not really be our problem. It is a problem for those folks living the old life in the North and South. I don't think we should change the ways of tradition. Families have been owning and trading slaves for 200 years. These folks, although owned by a master, are provided with good homes and work. Many of these owners educate the children and treat them as members of their own family. It is a better life than what might be expected if they were to all be set loose with no one to care. We should also not forget that the economy of the southern states has a solid foundation in this practice. A change in the system would affect all of the states and territories. And you too would find your life changed because of it. Think about it carefully.

Soon, election day will be here. I ask for your vote for a better and prosperous way of life. A vote for Melvin McClarin is a vote for a better tomorrow and truly a prosperous west. Thank you. I'll be looking for you on Election Day.

Melvin McClarin

Letter from a Politician for New Ideas

Letter from a Politican
for Tradition

My good citizens, you have heard the words of my distinguished colleague, Mr. Melvin McClarin. I am sure you will agree with me when I say that, although I acknowledge his verbose nature and his ability to put on a good campaign, I do not in any way support or agree with his ideas of what is best for our fine community.

Mr. McClarin supports an expansion of the railroad into this territory. Has he considered what it will bring into this community? Will we be inundated with a new breed of riffraff and undesirable characters? Consider the congestion and noise that will replace our quiet, friendly streets. Are we to forsake this upright community for the sake of monetary gain? Will our children and grandchildren be safe to follow the dreams and aspirations that we are so blessed with today?

Mr. McClarin has proposed to bring into this district two new teachers and provide traveling expenses on top of that. My question is, what of the fine, qualified young women right here in our town? Should it be necessary to go outside our boundaries when, may I say, we have our own charming and qualified candidates? They already know and understand the demographics of our small but growing town. I think that Mr. McClarin is more interested in spending the citizens' hard-earned money than educating our youth.

Finally, are we to be swindled by his southern mentality into supporting the ownership of other human beings? We cannot ignore the wickedness of this lifestyle. We must pride ourselves on our moral and righteous ethics. It is truly wrong to support and promote slavery, whether it exists here in our community or anywhere in this great nation.

We all must ensure that this expanding country is a better place to raise our children. If you truly desire this, cast your vote for me. Remember my name, Charles Frederick Hansford, a western man with western morality.

Charles Frederick Hansford
Your Next Mayor

Letter from a Politican for Tradition

Activity

In the days of the expanding West, political forums defined the direction of the growing nation. Individuals seeking power and control (civic or service) took to their platforms, and town halls became the center for debates on the issues that would later mold the face of the growing nation.

The Great Debate

Throughout his travels, the Cowboy encounters many individuals whose livelihoods are the direct result of political debate and majority vote. Ask your students to put themselves in the time period of our characters. Have them research the political conditions that existed in given places at given times. Ask them to debate the issues and present viable and valid reasons for their positions. Their goal is to persuade a voting constituent to support their position.

The letters from Melvin McClarin and Charles Frederick Hansford discuss a variety of issues. Topics that students can debate are:

* ★ Trapping animals for their fur as a commodity
* ★ The expansion of the railroad
* ★ Military involvement in the control of Native Americans
* ★ Allowing states to enter the Union as free or slave states
* ★ Putting another saloon in the community
* ★ Allowing sheep to graze on cattle land
* ★ Water or mineral rights

A variation on this activity is to have students present current political issues that are being debated at the national, state, or city level. Students can collect data from newspapers, call politician party headquarters, and contact local politicians for viewpoints on issues that affect their constituents.

Letter 18
Things Are Changing
in the Territories

I'll tell you, the election sure was exciting! The candidates really do believe in their points of view. You have to give them credit for running for public office. Although some folks only want more power, it appears obvious that many really want to do something good for the town and the new territory. It is so important that people get out and vote. Every man has that responsibility to determine the direction of our government, no matter how or what he believes. I hear tell that some women back in the Eastern states are talking about voting in the elections. It is strange how much things are changing. Women wanting to vote? It has never happened before, but this nation has been and is about change. It somehow doesn't seem right that women are excluded from this process. I can tell you so many stories about women helping to shape these territories with hard work, raising children and taking care of men, and many even giving their lives for what they believe in. I've seen women run cattle, drive wagons, hunt for food, build cabins, and lead settlers over mountain passes. They sure look equal to me! But that isn't yet the accepted way in this territory. I sure hope someday it will happen. I'll bet that cowgirl Savannah Rain will make it happen. I wonder if it will be in my lifetime.

Things Are Changing in the Territories

From *Galloping Along the Old West Trails* © 1996 Teacher Ideas Press 1-800-237-6124.

What was happening in this little town must have been important to someone because we had this fancy Eastern journalist here asking questions and more questions. He would ask even traveling folks like me what I thought of the slavery issue and the railroad right-of-way coming through town. I hear they write their articles and send them back east on a coach or with a very fast special horseback rider. Sometimes it takes weeks or even months before the writing appears in the big city newspaper or magazines.

I wonder if he will use my name, and if any of my friends near Quincy will see it. Sure would be nice, as no one other than you and my new friends have heard from me. Do you figure they think I'm all the way west, or dead? Or maybe they don't think about me at all, and life just goes on. What do you think about that? Have you ever had a friend move far away? Sometimes it makes me feel sad when I think about all those people back home. I'll write before I leave town. Good day.

Your friend,
The Cowboy

Things Are Changing in the Territories

From *Galloping Along the Old West Trails* © 1996 Teacher Ideas Press 1-800-237-6124.

Letter from an
Eastern Journalist

My name is Irwin Beadle. I am a journalist from the eastern part of this country. I am here in Kansas to discover how some of these cowboys live. You see, my brother Erastus, our business partner Robert Adams, and I have a publishing firm in New York. Have you ever heard of The House of Beadle and Adams? We publish stories about the West and the cowboys. People back east love reading everything they can get their hands on. Folks call these publications dime novels because that is what we sell them for. Others call them pulp novels because of the cheap quality paper we use. I don't care what they call them. All I know is that we are selling them faster than we can print them.

I meet cowboys every day and listen to their stories, and then I perhaps embellish them a bit. You see, a cowboy's life can be somewhat boring. If I told the public just how it really is on those cattle drives, no one would buy my books. But when I add to the stories a little excitement like a gunfight, a stampede, or a lovely lady to be saved, people think they're great.

For instance, just today, I met a cowboy riding a dapple gray quarter horse. What a fine animal that horse was. He would make a wonderful story just by

From *Galloping Along the Old West Trails* © 1996 Teacher Ideas Press 1-800-237-6124.

himself. I think his name was Kaper King (the horse, that is). Well, that cowboy looked a little tired, a bit underfed, and in need of a bath. His clothes were torn and worn. He had some interesting stories to tell, but well, they all do.

If I told his story, well, no one would be interested in reading it. So when I write a tale about this cowboy I'll probably entitle it something like "A Traveling Buckaroo and His Noble Steed Kaper King." I will describe him as a handsome buckaroo with a pure white hat and pure white leather chaps. His spurs will jingle as he rides atop that gallant horse. As he passes by the townspeople, he will politely tip his hat. Undoubtedly, he will run into some evil character and will have to save the town. The townspeople will be forever in his debt, but because he is such a honorable man, he will only say, "It's just part of bein' a cowboy." He will then ride off into the sunset.

Better story, don't you think? Anyway, save your dimes and remember, there is no finer character than the American cowboy. Just read about him and you will think so, too!

Irwin Beadle

Activity

The daily life of an ordinary cowhand was rather mundane. His day was long, and his job was tough. He rode atop a saddle all day and slept under the stars at night. All this, needless to say, could be quite tedious! This life was not what eastern journalists traveled west to write about.

They came looking for stories that would provide their readers with entertainment, excitement, and adventure. What they found was quite the opposite. But no problem. They just did what every good journalist of the day would do. They "embellished" upon the cowboy's deeds and "slightly" exaggerated the qualities of this western character. What the readers really wanted was a spruced-up romantic soul with a 10-gallon white hat and silver jingling spurs. Thus, the western cowboy was immortalized.

Such stories became known as dime novels. Printed on inexpensive paper, they were produced in mass. You could have your very own "authentic" story of the West for one single dime.

The Plot of a Dime Novel

As a language arts activity, have the students write and illustrate their own dime novels.

Instruct them to create characters that would have lived in the western era. The protagonist should have high moral character and be well respected by the townspeople. The horse should fit the character, as a fine noble steed. There should be an adversary in the story to create havoc or fear in the community. All should appear hopeless until the hero saves the day and does away with the "bad guys." (Just be careful that the kids don't stereotype the "weak" woman saved by the "brave" cowboy. You could suggest the students reverse the stereotyped gender roles—or show the pioneer woman and cowboy team up to outwit the "bad guys." This activity could be a good springboard for a discussion on gender equity.)

The writings should be full of description and dialogue. The readers must feel the soul of the hero or the heroine, so that when they read that he or she rides away into the sunset, there will be a burning desire to jump into the pages of the story and run behind and call, "Cowpoke, come back, come back!"

From *Galloping Along the Old West Trails*   © 1996   Teacher Ideas Press   1-800-237-6124.

Letter 19
Every Day Is Like
a Day at School

It is winter for sure! Brr! Glad I had a good warm bed in the town hotel last night. Maybe my last for some time. Can't stay here too long, or the money that I earned on the cattle drive will soon be gone. As we move farther from the cities, the prices keep getting higher. A good steak is still cheap, but clothes, shovels, picks, and other necessities are getting so expensive. Out here, people just keep fixing things rather than buying new ones. I guess that makes the most sense.

Checked out of the hotel and started off toward the stable to get Kaper King. Just off to the side of town, I noticed a small building with smoke coming from the chimney. Children were playing all around, and a lady, who must have been the teacher, was out front laughing and talking with the children. I thought I might as well take a shortcut by the schoolhouse and at the same time say hello to the children and young teacher. I said, "Howdy, ma'am," as I walked by the small one-room schoolhouse. She said, "Good morning, sir," with a pretty smile. Haven't been called "sir" in such a formal way in some time. She had a kind and friendly way about her. We talked for a moment, and I told her of my journey west. She invited me into the school as she called for the children to start the school day. Youngsters from about eight to fourteen years old scurried and pushed into the small building and took

Every Day Is Like a Day at School

their seats. The bigger students grabbed the higher desks while the small children took the little ones or sat in little squares on the floor. You could smell the wood burning in the corner iron stove, keeping the room warm and heating up water for morning tea and hot chocolate. It smelled so good and it seemed like such a safe place for the children ... and me.

This young teacher offered me some tea and hard cookies. That was nice, and the warm tin cup heated my chilled hands. The children were very good. Several of them asked why I was visiting, so I told them about my journey. Many of the children had friends or relatives that had ventured west. Most had not heard from them in a very long time.

It was time for school to begin, and they listened to the teacher and followed her directions. She would compliment them and smile when they did well. Even when the children didn't understand, she wouldn't lose her temper. She would look them in the eyes and continue until they showed a sense of new confidence. It had been nearly an hour. I don't know why I stayed as long as I did. Maybe because I felt hopeful as I watched those children—the future of our country — learn. The teacher asked me if I wanted to stay for lunch. It seems that the town's parents bring lunch to the teacher each day as a show of gratitude for what she does. I hear teachers don't get paid much, oftentimes only slightly more than the cost of their room and personal things. I thanked her and said I had to go and get my horse and be on my way.

She looked me in the eyes and said, "Good luck." I waved goodbye to her and the children and walked down the three wooden steps and across the muddy yard to a small bridge.

I imagined the children fishing behind the school when the water from the spring melt would flow. But soon now, it would be frozen over and still, sealing the small fish in until the thaw. Maybe I would return some day and see all these children grown up. Maybe I would even go fishing here. How fortunate they were to have such a nice teacher. Reminded me of some of the teachers that I had when I was in school. I thank God for those days that taught me so much about writing, great books, and history. Sometimes I think about my days as a young boy in school.

Well, I was sure Kaper King was waiting for me. Sure enough, his eyes brightened and his ears moved forward as he heard my whistle and saw my face appear from behind the stable doors. And, of course, Sierra wagged her blond tail as she too was ready for our journey to resume. Saddled up and off we went … just the three of us. Stay warm.

Your friends,
The Cowboy,
Kaper King, and
Sierra

Every Day Is Like a Day at School

My name is Miss Rebecca Cunningham, and I am the schoolteacher for this small community in Kansas. I teach in a one-room school. I have about 15 students on any given day, although some come on a more regular basis than others. This is because we are a farming community, and many of the children must help their parents when harvest time comes around. We learn reading, writing, and arithmetic. We do our lessons on slate with chalk. We must share books because we have so few. Many of my students do a fine job with their ABCs, numbers, and reading. Most read out of the Bible at home. The children are wonderful. Would you believe that some of my students are only a few years younger than I am, and many of the boys are much taller than me.

Today, a cowboy rode into town and visited our school. He was a friendly man with a big mustache. I could tell he had a kind heart. By his manner and speech I knew that he was an educated person. I often wonder why someone like that would take to being a cowboy ... such a lonely life. I guess his search for adventure takes him to many places. For me, I go to so many exciting places and meet wonderful characters every time I pick up a book. Reading can open up the world to us all.

In the spring I will be getting married, and I will no longer teach at this one-room school. You see, it is not proper for a married woman to work. I will miss this wonderful job and the beautiful children with their laughter, bright eyes, and inquisitive nature. One day my own children will be like these students, learning all that they can. I look forward to that time.

Watching the children acquire knowledge is the most rewarding experience a teacher can have. Ask your teacher if he or she agrees.

Sincerely,
Miss Cunningham

Activities

The soul of the cowboy was captured in the words he wrote and the songs he sang. His inspiration came from the world around him. It might have been the stars hanging overhead as he lay down by a dying fire, the sounds of the cattle in the morning dawn, or the rattling of the chuck wagon's pots and pans as it lumbered along the trail. Or maybe it was just the plain old dirt and loneliness that made him crazy enough to figure out something profound to say to anyone who would listen.

By Any Name, It's Poetry

Bring poetry to life for your students. Share aloud some cowboy poetry. Then introduce them to the "cinquain" poem.

First, review with them the format of a cinquain poem, noting the specific rules that apply to this simple five-line verse form. Demonstrate how a cinquain poem takes on a unique shape and form.

Cinquain

Line 1:   one two-syllable word that is the subject of the poem

Line 2:   four syllables describing the first line

Line 3:   six syllables showing action

Line 4:   eight syllables expressing an observation of the subject or telling of an expression of feeling

Line 5:   two syllables describing or renaming the subject

Sample Cinquain Poem:

Cowboy

Adventurous

Roping, Riding, Branding

Traveling the long Chisholm Trail

Lonely

Students can then write their own cinquain poems, using adjectives, verbs, and prepositional phrases that describe a selected theme based on events or feelings as related to the westward movement.

Discuss possible themes for the students to use in their poems. Perhaps play background music or display pictures of typical western scenes to generate ideas. An old pair of boots, spurs, or a saddle flung in the corner of the room may add to the experience. Our class took each character that was introduced by the Cowboy and developed poems based upon the distinctive lives of these individuals.

From *Galloping Along the Old West Trails*   © 1996 Teacher Ideas Press   1-800-237-6124.

There are a variety of ways to present the final product. We decided to use a computer writing program to type and format the poems. We photocopied the poems on parchment colored paper to give them an old, worn look and bound them in a book using construction paper that was first crinkled by hand to give the look of leather. Each student then proudly read the poem he or she had written. This makes for a nice memento of the experience and a fine addition to the Language Arts portfolio.

Spell 'em and Rope 'em

The mythology of the cowboy and his adventurous escapades is part of the image we have of the Old West. Out of this era came a lingo as unique as the characters themselves. Share examples with your students, then let them find, spell, pronounce, and define words that are associated with the cowboy and the West. (See page 110.)

The way you present weekly spelling and vocabulary lists will determine the procedure for incorporating this activity into your curriculum. Use these words for dictionary practice, journal entry writing, dramatic reading, word searches, crossword puzzles, and/or activity cards. The accompanying activity sheets can be used as you see fit.

You will find that your students will be ready to "rope them little doggies" with a 100 percent. Spell 'em, Rope 'em, Get 'long!

From *Galloping Along the Old West Trails* © 1996 Teacher Ideas Press 1-800-237-6124.

Spelling-Vocabulary List

1. buckaroo
2. roundup
3. longhorn
4. lasso
5. chaps

6. wrangler
7. cowhand
8. tenderfoot
9. range
10. cinch

11. rodeo
12. maverick
13. pinto
14. corral
15. cayuse

16. cowpoke
17. mustang
18. doggie
19. bulldog
20. brand

Vocabulary Test

| pinto | rodeo | longhorn | buckaroo | cinch |

1. _____ a spotted black or white or brown horse
2. _____ a contest of skill in roping cattle, riding horses and steers, etc.
3. _____ one of a breed of cattle with very long horns
4. _____ a strong strap for tightening the saddle
5. _____ a cowboy

| maverick | lasso | tenderfoot | brand | range |

6. _____ a calf or other animal not marked with an owner's brand
7. _____ a long rope used for catching cattle and horses
8. _____ a marking on cattle by hot irons
9. _____ someone new to the pioneer life of the western United States
10. _____ an open region over which livestock roam

| cowhand | chaps | cayuse | corral | roundup |

11. _____ a person who works on a cattle ranch
12. _____ a pen for horses, cattle, etc.
13. _____ strong leather trousers with no back
14. _____ an Indian-bred pony
15. _____ the act of driving or bringing cattle together

| wrangler | doggie | bulldog | mustang | cowpoke |

16. _____ a cowboy in charge of saddle horses
17. _____ a motherless calf
18. _____ to throw a steer by seizing the horns and twisting the neck
19. _____ a small wild horse of the North American plains
20. _____ slang for cowboy

From *Galloping Along the Old West Trails* © 1996 Teacher Ideas Press 1-800-237-6124.

I'm sleeping under the stars again tonight. As the chilly air settles, I hear only small critters scurrying close to the ground. Kaper King is tied to a "picket line," which is a long rope secured between two trees (it can also be secured to a couple of large rocks). Stretched tight, it is like a portable hitching rail. It works for one horse or thirty. Sometimes, though, all the horses start twitching and turning, and it's easy for them to get all tangled up. No problem with Kaper King, as he is the only one on the line and he's happy just being settled in for the night.

I hope you can picture our camp. Sierra is curled up next to me. We're probably keeping each other warm. I have a bedroll with a blanket that helps keep off the chill. I roll up my leather chaps to make a nice pillow, which sure takes the bumps out of the ground. We are camped up against a large rock outcropping. In this setting, the wind will be blocked and the wind chill will be reduced. If the wind starts blowing on a chilly winter night, a man can simply go to sleep and never wake up, just freeze to death right where he is. If it snows, no one will find him until the spring. That's why the blanket is around us, the huge rounded rocks are behind us, and the thick brush shelters us from all sides. Our small fire will burn most of the night, or at least the embers will emit some heat into the early hours of the morning.

It sure is dark out here. Only the stars peeking through the moving clouds give off a sparkle of light. I suppose some people would be scared out here, but what's there to be scared of? There are no other people, and certainly the animals will leave us alone. Kaper King, like most horses, only sleeps for 20 or 30 minutes at a time, so he is certainly quite alert to the movements and noises of the trail. I'm not sure about Sierra. She just seems content to be patted on the head and loved. Every now and then she will hear a sound and run off into the night, barking and howling. I suppose it's only a shadow or a jackrabbit. It makes me feel better knowing that there are three of us now.

Good night,
The Cowboy

Just Normal Things

Activity

When I first thought about going west, I simply envisioned myself and my good ole horse crossing green valleys, drinking from crystal clear streams, and eating freshly hunted meat by a crackling fire. Soon I would discover that it is the weather that decides if you're going to make it. On those many freezing nights and blistery hot days, the weather and I reached an understanding. I learned that I couldn't reason with it.

The Weather West

We can only count on a few things in life, one of which is the weather. It will always rain, the wind will blow, and sometimes it will be so hot that the air conditioner knows that it is time to quit. Knowing this, like our cowboy moving west, we need to learn to "understand the weather." The weather is always exciting, particularly when it's raining buckets and you have 35 students glued to the windows. Adults are fascinated with the weather, so why shouldn't kids be? Channel this excitement into a learning opportunity using your ... secret weather box!

Inside this box is everything you need to teach a great weather lesson—while it's actually happening!

Prior to the next rainy school day you will need to assemble the contents of your secret weather box. You will need to purchase some of the equipment. The students can construct other equipment or borrow things from home. You will need:

* thermometers
* barometers
* wind velocity meters
* paper, pencils, and crayons for drawing
* paper for charting and graphing
* butcher paper for murals
* lined paper for writing

Be sure to review the following components of this activity at least once before you do it with the class. Directions and organization are important parts of this activity as it involves the concept of group responsibility. Be sure to review cooperative group learning. Then, get ready to designate tasks for each group member and explore the wonderful world of weather!

Rain gauges. Look up in a good science book how to make a rain gauge. Remember to put the receptacle several feet above the ground so the splash doesn't fill the gauge, distorting the actual measurement. You can have one group responsible for checking the rainfall each hour of the day. Graphing and charting are naturals for this activity.

Thermometers. Another group can check the temperature on an hourly basis (they will need to go outside to do this). Again charting, graphing, and reporting to the class can be an hourly activity.

Activity

113

Barometric pressure. Using an inexpensive barometer, show the students how they can track the barometric pressure as the storm passes through. Keeping records of these data and reporting them is what science is all about. This is also a good activity for predicting weather patterns daily; have students chart the barometric pressure over several days or weeks.

Wind velocity. Try to make a small wind velocity meter (the little vertical propeller with the small cups on each stick). Well balanced, it represents the speed of the wind outside of your classroom.

Cloud observation. Still another group can observe the clouds as they develop for the advancing storm. The observation group can actually draw the type of clouds they see and the changes that appear over a designated period of time. Drawings can be posted in chronological order.

Reporting to the class. After data collection is complete, each group will report to the class their findings. If the storm continues, the weather groups can rotate responsibilities the following day. Have fun and stay dry.

Hot chocolate. There is nothing like hot chocolate and cookies on a rainy day.

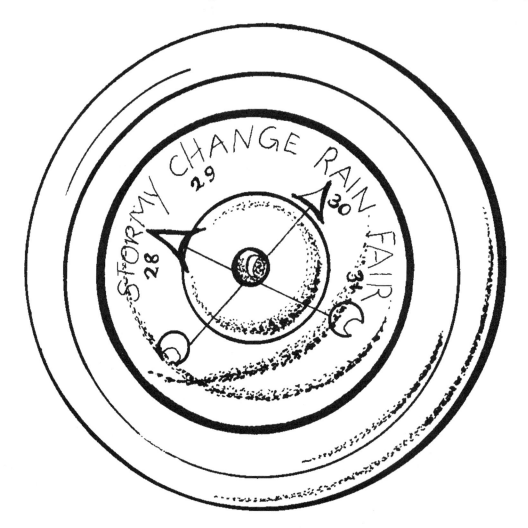

BAROMETER

Activity

Letter 21
The Next Morning

Had some dried meat, stale crackers, and water for breakfast. That sustained me until we got to the next town. I caught a few very slow lizards the afternoon before and cooked them over the fire and fed them to Sierra for breakfast. She's not too particular and doesn't seem to want to do her own searching for food. She's not exactly a great hunting dog.

Cleaned up the campsite and saddled up. The three of us were on the trail again. It is a little sad to look back at that campsite and think that we will never see it again. I don't ever want to forget that each place where we stay and each person whom we meet gives us a little something to take with us on our journey.

We will stop at the town up ahead and get a few more supplies. I heard that a wagon train is starting up again, and they want more men to join the party. The more people, the safer it seems. It certainly wouldn't hurt me to be with more folks as we travel through the winter.

Coming into town, can't remember the name, but I thought it might be something like Ogallala. Funny name—must have come from one of the lizards Sierra finished off for breakfast. The town was small with wood facades, raised wooden walkways in front of the stores, and, of course, a muddy main street. I was concerned that the mud would create a suction that would surely pull off the shoes of my fine horse, Kaper King. Darn, sure as flies land on honey, we lost the left back

From *Galloping Along the Old West Trails* © 1996 Teacher Ideas Press 1-800-237-6124.

shoe. I'll head toward the blacksmith around the corner to see if he can fashion a new shoe for Kaper King.

He said he would have no trouble accommodating us. I noticed a beautiful fire-hardened hand ax with a strong wooden handle on the table. I would need such a tool for my travels, and I asked if the blacksmith had made that ax and whether it was for sale. With pride he smiled, and said yes. One could tell by looking at that blade that it was made with the heart, and it would do something special someday. Maybe it would cut up wood for fire in a snowstorm or trim the rough edges from timber that would become a good house. It just seemed as if that ax had a special purpose. I paid six bits for it and two for the shoe, and thanked the blacksmith for something in my future even though I wasn't quite sure what it would be.

I walked Kaper King down the street and tied him to the hitching post in front of the general store. I pulled each of my feet from the thick mud, finally stepping up on the splintering walkway. I told Sierra to "mind the horse" and to stay where she was until I got back. She looked at me with those brown eyes and wagged her tail. I opened the door of the shop and stepped out of the cold. I'll write again soon.

The Cowboy and
His Friends

The Next Morning

Letter from the Blacksmith

My name is Ervin, and I'm often the first person up and around in town in the early morning. I need to fire up my stone fireplace, often called a stove or hearth. I need to get my tools organized and my fire burning hot so that the coals are red and fierce when I begin my work. I am the town blacksmith and have been at it since this town was but a speck on the map to Oregon.

You may be wondering what a blacksmith does. Some people confuse the blacksmith with the fellow who puts shoes on horses. That's not me, although in an emergency I've done that too. I actually do what has to be done with iron. I make tools such as ax blades, shovels, hoes, hammers, cooking pots, vats, and other utensils. You can't build the West without the nails that I make with steel, heat, my hammer, and my anvil. Imagine if we had no blacksmith and no nails. It would be tough keeping all those buildings up with string. Ha ha. You can probably think of lots more things that a blacksmith makes. If it is made from iron I either make it or repair it. People out here don't throw away broken tools. If you have a horse plow with broken blades, you load it up on your wagon, and when in town, you drop it off at my shop for repair. I try to do quality work, knowing that a man's livelihood may depend on it. A farmer can't till the earth if his plow breaks in the field. A woodsman can't cut timber if his ax breaks during a hard swing. And it is dangerous if one of these tools should break. I think you get the idea. Anyway, let me explain a little bit about how I work with the iron to make and repair what I call "the tools of the West."

After the fire is at its hottest, I set in pieces of iron and heat them until they turn almost white. Once a piece of iron is hot, I remove it from the fire and work it as it cools. Holding it with special tools, I rest it on the heavy anvil and begin to bend, twist, pound, and shape it. The anvil is a very heavy block of iron, one end pointed and the other end more of a square. Mine has some holes in it so that I can insert smaller pieces of iron for bending. I bought my anvil in St. Louis.

You can imagine the hazards of working with hot metal. I wear heavy overalls and a long-sleeve shirt and gloves to protect myself from the burning pieces of iron that may chip off during the forming process. Even with all the safety precautions, I still have had some accidents that have left scars on my arms and face.

The work is long and hard, hot and noisy, but I like it because I'm making quality tools and because I help people repair what they need to live. In the evening, when the amber sun is setting behind the rolling hills and the fireplace is cooling, I often wonder if the West would ever have been settled without the blacksmiths like me. Interesting thought.

Well, enough for today. If you should be in these parts soon, you listen for the "ping, ping, ping" of my hammer and come by for a visit.

Blacksmith Ervin

Letter from the Blacksmith

From *Galloping Along the Old West Trails* © 1996 Teacher Ideas Press 1-800-237-6124.

Activities

According to the blacksmith, it was men like him who really built the West, with a blazing fire in the hearth, the pounding of white hot steel, the molding of raw iron. It was hot, dirty, and dangerous work.

Foiling Around

Have students construct utensils and tools that the western Blacksmith might have forged. Cut a foot or more of heavy aluminum foil for each student. Students may fold, twist, turn, or cut the foil to shape miniature tools or products of the west. Let them try their hand at plows, pitchforks, shovels, wheelbarrows, hooks, and latches.

An Iron Scavenger Hunt

Have the students, in cooperative groups, walk around your classroom or school making lists of all the items they can find that could have been made by a blacksmith in the 1850s. From their findings, generate a classroom list of all the items and post them on the board. Compare the results of each group and tally the findings. From these numbers, create mathematical graphs and tables. Reward the group with the most items with a delicious piece of chocolate candy, wrapped in aluminum foil, of course!

Where Is the Blacksmith?

Find a local iron shop, and have your students compare Ervin the Blacksmith with the metalworker of today. If you can't take your class on a field trip to a metal shop, ask the proprietor if *you* can videotape the activities of the facility to share later with your class. It should make for an interesting discussion.

From *Galloping Along the Old West Trails* © 1996 Teacher Ideas Press 1-800-237-6124.

Letter 22
Candy in My Pocket

I walked from where the chilled wind was blowing and the rain was rushing through the streets like it was an arroyo. The harsh weather would rage for an hour, then magically disappear and dry up in a matter of minutes. I was sorry to have to leave Sierra and Kaper King out there, but I wouldn't be long in the general store.

I opened the wooden door and felt the warm air hit me as I stepped over the threshold. The cold melted away from my face, and the water droplets fell from my mustache. The store was sweet smelling like the fancy downtown shops of St. Louis. The store was filled with all sorts of things, some of which I had never seen before. Bags and bottles, bins and shelves all filled with merchandise that mothers and fathers, sisters and brothers, explorers and settlers would need at some time or another.

Behind the counter was a lady who was sure a pleasant sight on a cold morning. She was the proprietor of the shop. I must have been staring, for she stood right in front of me and said, "Hey, Cowboy, can I help you with something?" I said, "Sure, ma'am," and I began to look for the items that I either needed for my journey or I wanted just because I wanted them!

I needed a couple of pounds of oats for Kaper King and some dried meat for those meals when you can't build a fire. I found a bin of biscuits that would be nice for Sierra. Some ground coffee would be good on the trail and a bag of hard

Candy in My Pocket

From *Galloping Along the Old West Trails* © 1996 Teacher Ideas Press 1-800-237-6124.

candy. I put some of that candy in my pocket so I'd have it when the need arose. I love a sweet piece of hard candy once in a while. I asked the shopkeeper if she had any dried and salted fish, but she said she never really cared for it, so she just didn't carry it in the store. I guess it's a taste or texture you either grow up with or get used to. Living near the Mississippi, I had fish often, and it seemed quite natural.

I went over to the counter and set down all the items I was to buy with my cattle drive money. The lady shopkeeper counted the items, added the prices, and carefully handed each purchase to me to place in my saddlebags. I gave her the coins, and she warmly said good-bye and wished us luck on our journey. She asked me if I was to join the wagon train, and I answered, "Yes, for a while." I thanked her for her good wishes. She became another person who touched my life, one whom I would never see again. I pondered that thought for a moment, and then it was time to go.

I really didn't want to step out into that cold, but I opened the door and out I went. I gave Kaper King a handful of oats. I patted each of them in a special way. We walked down the street, three odd traveling companions looking for the wagon train.

The Cowboy

Candy in My Pocket

From *Galloping Along the Old West Trails* © 1996 Teacher Ideas Press 1-800-237-6124.

Letter from the Shopkeeper

I'm about to open the doors of the shop for business on this chilly morning. Through the door shade, I can see Mrs. Hopkins and Mrs. Cannel waiting on the boardwalk. The fire in my corner iron stove is emitting a warmth around my shop that I hope will take the chill off of my customers and friends when they visit.

You could say this was the one and only general store in town. I try to carry all of the goods and supplies folks might need for housekeeping, cooking, and farming. I try to have items for settlers staying on here in town, as well as for those just stocking up as they pass through. I always have a full cookie jar for the children who stop by with their parents. I like it here. Nice people and a fine town. I like it when lots of folks step out of the chill and gather in the shop for conversation, gossip ... and if they buy a few things, all the better.

During the winter, it is more difficult to get the goods that we need, so I encourage people to stock up on things in the fall and spring. Most folks listen to me as I've been in this business for quite a few years now. Remember, also, that many of the townspeople who shop here don't live right in town. Some live as far as 30 miles in all directions. That sometimes requires a two- or three-day ride to town, and in the worst winter weather it is an impossible journey. I hear that in parts of California it doesn't snow at all any time of the year. Maybe that's why so many people are headed that way. Actually, it's for the gold in the hills. No one would move all the way across the country just to escape a little rough weather.

I try to be a good citizen of the town and help people when they have a run of bad luck. Usually one or two families a year ask me for credit for supplies needed for the farm. I try to help the best I can. I've never been disappointed as they are always at my door as soon as the harvest comes in. I do remember one time when Harvey Potter asked me for credit to buy seed and tools for his new crop. Harvey was a bit peculiar but an honest man. He had some bad luck and needed a hand. Didn't hear from him, but that's not unusual as he lived nearly 40 miles to the west. Two years went by, and I had almost forgotten about the debt when I heard from a stranger that Harvey must have been knocked unconscious when cutting wood for the winter. A storm came through and Harvey just froze right there with his ax in his hand. Just thought you might want to know that life can be tough. So can death.

Being a good business person, I learned quickly that trading things with folks was good business and helped everyone. I will trade clothing, jam, honey, and wood utensils. I have a couple of fine polished wooden boxes on my shelf that I got from Sam Lorde in exchange for a 50-pound bag of flour. I try to be fair, and I am treated fairly in return. I forgot to mention that I have an old wagon and strong horse out back, and we do make deliveries within a reasonable distance from town. Folks appreciate that, especially those getting on in years. I know Mrs. Hopkins will want to see that new catalogue I just received in the mail from Boston. They've got some mighty pretty things in there. The catalogue company said it can rush deliver ordered items in only eight weeks. I'm sure we are going to have some people waiting in lines to look through those fine books.

I think I'll go over to the stove, make myself and the others a good cup of spice tea, and begin the day. Nice chatting with you, and stop by the store if you ever need anything. Even candy!

Della Dansbury

Letter from the Shopkeeper

123

Activities

The general store in an old western town was the link to the world outside the community. Here the townspeople could purchase those items they could not produce themselves. Items from A to Z could usually be found in barrels, on the shelves, or in gunnysacks leaning against the walls.

Everyone who lived in the community eventually passed through the doors of the general store. They came with money in their pockets, goods to exchange, or the character to guarantee credit on their purchases. With a good mind for numbers, purchases could be had at reasonable and fair prices.

Let's Go Shopping

Explain to the students the value of the dollar in 1850 versus its value today. Discuss the wages of workers then and now.

Tell the students that they each have $100 to spend. Instruct them to make a list of things they could buy today for that amount. Then have them list purchases they could make in the 1850s. They will feel quite wealthy by the time they finish this inventory.

Conversions

Have the students make lists of items in the general store that fit the following categories:

- ★ Sold by inches, feet, or yards (e.g., fabric, rope, barbed wire, wooden plank, or chain)
- ★ Sold by pints, quarts, or gallons (e.g., preserves, paint, glue, ointments)
- ★ Sold by ounces or pounds (e.g., candy, sugar, flour, seed)

To extend this activity: Using a conversion chart, have the students create problems that employ conversion applications. An example would be:

Mrs. Lingerman wanted to purchase calico fabric to sew a new dress. She needed 144 inches to make the dress. How many yards did she buy?

Stock the Shelves

Selling merchandise was the top priority for the owner of the general store. It was important to display the merchandise in such a way that the customer would be tempted to purchase the goods. Using the following list, have the students determine the best way to display and place merchandise in the store. The students should explain their reasoning. Perhaps they could make illustrations of the general store showing the placement of these items.

* flour
* grease
* sugar
* candy
* preserves
* fruit
* onions
* rope
* lumber
* nails
* water barrels
* ax
* shovel
* flower seeds
* fence wire
* shoes
* fabric
* lace
* buttons
* thread
* needles
* watches
* mail order catalogs
* dishes
* canvas

You may want the students to work in cooperative groups on this activity. They can experience working with a "business partner." They might discover that joint decision making, cooperation, and compromise are important tools for ensuring success in a prospering company (or, on the other hand, that this approach could lead to financial ruin). Their final grade will seal the fate of their general store.

From *Galloping Along the Old West Trails*   © 1996   Teacher Ideas Press   1-800-237-6124.

Letter 23
With the Wagon Train

I've been with the wagon train for a week now, and traveling is slower than expected. About 20 wagons, oxen, horses, mules, and an assortment of other carts are making their way west. We have had some breakdowns, which is lowering the morale of the group. Although I am new to this train, many have been with it since it left the east four months ago. They thought, or hoped, to be much farther along by now. Some have turned back, others have just homesteaded where their wagons broke down, and a few have found new destinations.

Today, two axles cracked, so more time was lost while they were repaired. Where the axle meets the wheel should be filled with grease. But these harsh traveling and weather conditions are so difficult that the grease often slips out or dries up, particularly if people forget to attend to it. I volunteered to ride to a small town to see about filling our "grease horns" with fresh lubricant for the wheels. A grease horn is an essential item for any wagon. Not to have full horns is just inviting trouble. The others told me not to hurry as they had plenty to do. I think it was time to check each wagon and make any needed repairs before we headed out on the trail. I found some grease horns at the livery stable, had them filled with black grease, and secured the caps on each. I lashed them to my saddle and began to ride out of town when I saw it! Right on the corner of the wooden building was a sign that said in big, bold letters "Hot Bath." A real bathhouse with hot

With the Wagon Train

water! Washing out of a pan with cold water or taking a sponge bath from a pot of water heated over an open fire isn't the same as a hot bath. No, sir, it isn't.

I went back to the livery stable, paid for a dry stall for Kaper King, removed his tack, took some clean clothes from my pack, and walked with authority right to the front door of that bathhouse. One hour later, I emerged a different man. Clean shaven, free from dust and mud, I could have been mistaken for a real city dude. The cost of the bath and razor shave, some good smelling cologne, and my clean clothes might have seemed wasted not going any place special. But I'll tell you, it sure felt good. I knew Kaper King would appreciate it, too! It was a relaxing ride back to the camp as I sang an old cowboy song taught to me by one of the men on the trail crew. I don't have much of a voice, but Kaper King didn't seem to mind much ... or at least he didn't say anything.

We arrived back at the camp about the time the sun was just dipping below the horizon. We spent the next two hours greasing all the wagon wheels from those horns. I wasn't so clean anymore, but I sure felt good inside. Tomorrow we will be moving along again.

Your friend,
The Cowboy

With the Wagon Train

From *Galloping Along the Old West Trails* © 1996 Teacher Ideas Press 1-800-237-6124.

Activity

The songs of the cowboy added character to the ever-growing legend of this rugged man. The verses sung told of his lonely life, his love for the land he roamed, and the fortitude of his pioneering spirit.

A Cowboy Serenade

Check the public library, nearest music store or local children's bookstore for tapes, CDs, or sheet music (if you can play a musical instrument) containing some of these "oldies but goodies":

- ★ "Home on the Range"
- ★ "The Streets of Laredo"
- ★ "I'm Going to Leave Old Texas"
- ★ "Sweet Betsy of Pike"
- ★ "My Home's in Mountains"
- ★ "Red River Valley"
- ★ "The Old Chisholm Trail"
- ★ "Shenandoah"
- ★ "Good-bye Ol' Paint"

Students can sing the songs around a campfire (or, in the classroom, a battery-operated lamp with the overhead lights off). Later, they can illustrate the verses to create big books that can be shared with the school.

Here are a couple of song books that contain appropriate songs:

- ★ Beall, Pamela Conn, and Susan Hagen Nipp. *Wee Sing America.* Los Angeles: Price Stern Sloan, 1987.
- ★ Moon, Dolly M. *My First Book of Cowboy Songs.* Mineola, NY: Dover Publications, 1982.
- ★ *Songs of the Wild West.* Commentary by Alan Axelrod. Arrangements by Dan Fox. New York: Metropolitan Museum of Art, Simon & Schuster, 1991.

Letter 24
Sadness and Progress
on the Trail West

The wagon train is moving again, but it continues to be slow going. We have been plagued by more breakdowns and heartaches. Yesterday, a wagon tipped over on its side and was torn to bits when it drifted into a fast current while we were fording a river. No one aboard was seriously hurt, but the family was left with nothing. No food, clothes, tools, or money. All washed down that raging river. Some of the other folks took them in and offered whatever help they could, but I hear that they will be leaving the train tomorrow so as not to be a burden. However, that is not the worst. Fever is spreading through the camp, with six people in three different families coming down with the sweats and shaking. It doesn't look good. Medicine is in scarce supply, and no one really knows what this ailment is. The wagon boss told me that the party will be staying here until things get better. He said that it could be days or even weeks. "No point in going on while people are sick and vulnerable to accidents," he said.

It was with sadness that I decided to say good-bye to the nice folks who had become my friends. I would leave the wagon train and travel on by myself (of course taking Kaper King and Sierra with me). That night, I left some of my dried meat in the wagon of the family that was sick and gave a few coins to the folks who lost their wagon in the river. I wished I could have done more, but I needed my remaining money and supplies to make the next leg of the journey. I hope I will find more work, but one never knows for sure.

Sadness and Progress on the Trail West

129

In the morning, I said a heartfelt good-bye and rode away down the trail, looking back to see the small circle of wagons disappear in the distance. The fever going through the wagon train really bothered me. I had heard of fever spreading from the settlers to the Indians and entire tribes of peaceful people dying inside of three days. I could only hope and pray that this would not be the case and that the fever would be under control very soon.

The land was flat with occasional rolling hills. This was farmland that had been crudely worked by settlers deciding to make this their new home. I had talked to some of the farmers. They work hard, never knowing whether this will be the year they will go hungry or the year they will take a fine harvest crop to market. This time of year they had stored much of what was grown and harvested at the end of summer and beginning of fall. Cold storage isn't too difficult out here. Can you figure out why that is? Maybe one of those farmers will contact you. If I should hole up for a few days at one of those farms, perhaps we can write you all a letter. It sure is nice that we can stay in touch during my journey west. It makes me feel like I have a special family.

The days are now a bit longer, and the sun is truly beginning to warm all the living creatures. Could this be the beginning of spring? Kaper King is more energetic and Sierra is venturing farther from the trail, chasing whatever she can. I don't know what she would do if she ever caught up with anything.

The Cowboy and
My Companions

Letter from the Farmer

My mail is addressed to Lionel Parker, and I'm proud to be a farming man with my family in the Nebraska territory. The soil here was found to be as rich as the gold being dug from the hills of California. This is God's country. The skies are clear and blue, the land is flat and rich, and the spirit of the settlers is friendly and sharing. Hadn't planned on making this our home, but after running my fingers through the soil, I knew my wagon had rolled as far as it was going to.

We had no proper equipment when we first arrived, so we used what they once called a light iron plow. This tool turned the soil as it was either pulled by animal or man. It was slow compared with what we needed, but that's all we had. Those first months, we worked an hour before the sun came up to an hour after the sun set. I remember coming in to see my wife, Rose, staring at me and laughing. I was literally covered with dirt from the top of my head to my feet. I guess it was a funny sight. Later we were able to borrow a sod-busting plow, which would cut the earth deeper and turn the soil over, leaving a smooth pattern.

When several of the farmers met one evening that first year in the fall, we pooled our money and resources and began to share equipment. We plowed, pulling our equipment with our horses, and we raked the clods with another pass. We were now ready to plant our first crop, which of course you know was corn. I can still see the smooth brown earth before the planting and the paradise of the green ocean of plants just before the harvest. We dance with joy when the bounty is great, but we mourn with sorrow when locusts or drought steal away the glory. Some farmers have given up and returned east, while others have moved west in search of a

From *Galloping Along the Old West Trails*   © 1996   Teacher Ideas Press   1-800-237-6124.

better and easier way of life. When the duststorms come, we can do nothing but wait until the ocean of pain recedes.

Those first two years, the family took pride in planting the corn. One of us would dig out a small hole, one of the children would drop in a few corn kernels, the next person would fill the hole, and the final person would tamp it down. The process would repeat itself, day in and day out until our hands and backs were sore from the stooping. Finally the last hole was filled and we stood back with pride ... and waited.

The first year, the rain did come. That year, our new corn thrust itself from the damp ground. The second year, the rains were slow and the summer heat and winds blew the earth away. The third year was again good. We had learned much from our short stay in our new home.

Then came the fourth year. Everything seemed perfect. The crop was the best ever, and we were already dreaming of the money that would be raised from the harvest sale. I remember that it was about two in the afternoon, and we were sipping cool water by the sod wall near the barn. We looked out across the fields to see a gray cloud in the distance. The cloud grew and the dark wings enveloping it signaled the disaster that was upon us. The deafening sound of voracious grasshoppers overtook everything in its path. Our dreams of bounty were leveled in but a few hours. The storm of grasshoppers passed, and the bright sun shone, but we were standing in a strange and barren land once again.

It's been six years now, and we have some cattle, some sheep, and a small herd of working horses. Our house is now made mostly of wood, and our fine barn is the center of activity. I still love the mornings when the sun is coming up from the east and I can smell the new day in the calm air. I look up to the sky and wonder what will be coming today.

Lionel Parker

Letter from the Farmer

Activity

A hundred years ago, anyone could have a ranch, a farm, or certainly a garden. In today's world of blacktop and manicured lawns, we often forget about the wonderful vegetable garden and the values it fosters.

Where Have All the Flowers, Radishes, and Carrots Gone?

Share the fun of a classroom vegetable garden with your students. It's not as difficult as you might think.

If you already have a planter outside your classroom, check to see if the plants are worth saving. If not, rip them out, insert wooden stakes at all four corners of the planter, and fasten string from stake to stake. If you are disturbing the existing grass, strike a deal with the principal that you will establish a modest garden, and when finished, the students will either replant using grass seed or install sod.

If no decent earth is available, solicit donations of old wood from a local lumberyard. Try to get boards 8 to 12 inches high, ½ inch to ¾ inches wide, and as long as they'll give you. Lay out the boards in a large rectangle on the dirt or asphalt and connect the corners so you have a large frame. This frame will delineate your raised vegetable garden. Fill it with soil, planter mix, or mulch and you will have a very productive garden.

The students can select the "veggies" they want to plant. You will be surprised how involved they will become in this project. You can integrate science, social studies, and ecology activities. The students can even sing songs and do art.

Activity

133

Letter 25
On the Trail
Following Along the River

We are making good time again, although we are by
ourselves. That is Kaper King, Sierra, and me. What would
you call the three of us if you were to see us on the trail?
Sometimes, days go by between towns, so we usually stop at
them all unless one doesn't seem safe. A few towns are
havens for outlaws and the rules of the West don't seem to
apply there (or maybe these are the rules of the West).
Best to stay clear of those places.
     Today we came across a small rustic enclave or what is
the beginnings of a town. We saw an interesting sight when
we happened by the town square. A group of people were
standing in a small circle outside of the newspaper office
pointing excitedly to the newsprint tacked up to the wall.
Because many people couldn't read, they would hang around
the newspaper office, and when the editor tacked up the
paper, someone would read the news to those who were
interested. I tied Kaper King to a hitching post, told Sierra
to sit, and sauntered over to the gathering crowd. My word!
Now I understood what the commotion was about. A man by
the name of Buchanan had been elected the 15th President
of the Union. I wonder what the future would hold now that
he would be the new President.
     As well, people were talking excitedly about the Utah
War, in which 120 settlers were massacred. I guess I'll need

From *Galloping Along the Old West Trails* © 1996 Teacher Ideas Press 1-800-237-6124.

to be sure things are calm before I ride too close to the Utah territory.

One other article in the paper talked about the reoccurrence of the deadly measles outbreak of 1847. Some say, that after 10 years, it will strike again. I'm not so sure about that. Maybe someday, we will have some strong medicine that will keep people from getting these killer diseases. That would truly be a miracle.

The editor of the paper came out on the sidewalk, and the townspeople had all kinds of questions for him. I would imagine it is an interesting job, gathering up the news and sharing it with people all over the country.

The geography of the area is changing. My map must have been lost some days past. I hope you can find me on your map and tell me if I'm in for a hard ride. I'll be writing again soon. My best to all of you.

Your friend,
The Cowboy

Letter from the
Newspaper Editor

James Smidley is the name, and I am the town newspaper editor. My office is across the street. Behind those doors you will find my new press right off the wagon from Boston. It took 10 months for that sweet piece of iron to arrive, and when it did, this little town came of age. With my assistant, we now spend fewer hours every week getting the paper out. We can print the paper much faster ... a newspaperman's dream come true! What an invention it is!

I love the smell of the fresh black newsprint after the weekly run. I spend a week in and around the territory, talking with new people in town, interviewing those in the community, and writing the editorials. I have a reporter who is always busy on one story or another. Things are changing so fast, and although news is often slow arriving, it is happening faster than we can write it down. These are exciting times indeed.

Our town isn't like the cities in the East where newspapermen compete for the story and become ruthless in their desire to win readers. Here, I'm the only paper in town, and I see it as my duty to provide a good paper, one that tells people what is going on, for a fair price. As well, I enjoy writing the editorials giving my opinions related to the many new developments occurring in the West. Over the past few months I have written and printed editorials on subjects as diverse as Prohibition, the railroad, banking, cattle ranching, sheep herding, and religion. I hope my editorials will get the people of our town thinking and motivate

From *Galloping Along the Old West Trails* © 1996 Teacher Ideas Press 1-800-237-6124.

them to become involved in the answers as well as the questions.

I feel it is so important for people to be informed that we post every run of our paper outside the office so that those who can't afford their own copy can still read the news. And for those folks who don't know how to read, there is usually someone reading the paper aloud, and a wonderful discussion usually follows. Sometimes the discussion carries over into the saloon. That usually makes for a lively evening.

When an issue comes up that the people need to know about, it is my responsibility to make sure that the paper provides information that will help them understand both sides of the issue. At the same time I write editorials offering my personal views on the issues. I often invite a guest editor to write his or her views as well. Our paper is growing quickly, and we now have regular columns on "New Products in the East," "People on the Prairie," "Washington Ways," and "Best Recipes." It's a good life working for the paper. I always know what's happening.

If you're in the territories, whether you have news or not, stop by the newspaper office and I'll show you around. We're talking about beginning to deliver papers to folks in town. I'm not sure if that's an idea that will catch on. I guess we'll just have to look into it.

James Smidley
Editor

Activity

As the Cowboy and other settlers moved west, contact with relatives and the news of the country became scarce. Newspapers began to spring up in the new territories both as a poetic tabloid, as well as a connection to the life left behind. On the day of a new edition (few newspapers were dailies), you could see the townspeople gathered around the newspaper office listening to the newspaper being read. There was always excitement in the air as debate and discussion followed the reading.

North, East, West, and South: Creating a Classroom Newspaper

Working in cooperative groups, students can create their own newspaper of the West. Information can come from the letters received from the Cowboy and the other western characters. As the students receive correspondence, have them write newspaper articles based on these communiqués.

Have groups verify information and historical events using classroom and school libraries, reference materials and textbooks. Research famous and infamous historical personalities of the given time period. Format newspaper articles based on these true-to-life stories. If the technology is available, access on-line telecommunication services and explore encyclopedias, magazines, museums, and other databases.

Once the students have written their articles, they are ready to format a newspaper. This can be done either manually (cut and paste articles and art work), or by using a software program. Photocopy the finished piece.

Distribute the newspaper to students, parents, the principal, and anyone else the children deem appropriate. Don't forget grandparents and, of course, the superintendent.

Letter 26
A Soldier and an Artist

Another beautiful day on the trail. Still a bit chilly, but warming up with each sunrise. Still following the big river. This one, whose name I can't remember, is not like the mighty Mississippi. Here in places the white water runs so fast it could break wagons to splinters and carry men to their deaths if they were to lose control while crossing in the most treacherous parts. Up ahead, the river swings back over the trail, so we will have to ford the river to get to the other side. I can see a couple of wagons and some riders on horseback by the river's edge. They must be waiting for enough people to arrive to help each other with the crossing.

A couple of families were camped out by the shore, along with a soldier on his way to join his regiment at Fort Laramie and a minister who was to join a new parish. While we were waiting, an artist set up his easel and sketched this picturesque scene. He told me his name was Albert Bierstadt. Sounds like a European name to me. He sure had a fine hand for art. A thousand miles away, one could look at his picture and almost hear the rushing water and feel the wind blowing down the canyon walls.

The next morning we crossed the river. It took nearly four hours to get everyone from shore to shore, but with ropes and pulleys and some shouting and hootin', we all made it to the other side. It is amazing how quickly you get to know people on the trail. The soldier invited me for a

---

A Soldier and an Artist   139

meal at the fort if I should end up there. I thanked him and said it was very possible.

I forgot to mention that I put Sierra across my saddle in front of me while fording the river. She looked rather worried, but she didn't have to swim, nor did I have to worry that she would be carried away in the fast current. When we rode up on the shore, she jumped down and ran ahead over the next hill, wagging her tail all the way.

Again soon,
The Cowboy

A Soldier and an Artist

Activity

In *The Watercolors of William Matthews*, this contemporary artist brings the cowboy and the images of the West to life. Matthews is just one of many talented artists to document on canvas the western legend. Such greats as Frederic Remington, Charles Marion Russell, Edward Borein, Carl Rungius, William Henry Koerner, and Charles Schreyvogel have immortalized the cowboy with the stroke of the brush and forever imprinted his image into the American consciousness.

The Artists: Remington and the Rest

Bring the drama of cowboy art into the classroom. Students can re-create paintings and drawings of the great American artists who documented the West, using crayons, watercolors, markers, paints, and charcoal.

Locate photographs and prints of famous paintings by the artists mentioned above. Check out books and prints from local libraries, download pictures from on-line telecommunication services, or seek out anyone you know who might have visual aids to enhance this lesson.

Display one of the selected art pieces in a prominent location in the classroom. Discuss the art composition, color, and design. Ask students to re-create the art piece using the materials provided them. You might also want to present this lesson as directed drawing, taking the children step by step through the construction of the art piece.

When the students have completed their "masterpieces," they can sign them (on the front lower corner), mat them and proudly display them in their own "Western Art Gallery."

(As the children paint and draw, let them smell a tangy western stew slowly simmering in a slow cooker pot in the corner of the classroom. Play a variety of authentic western music including that of the great American composer Aaron Copland.)

Activity   141

Letter 27
Tracks in Both Directions

We've been following some tracks made in the caked mud as we make our way still farther west. The terrain has changed significantly, and we are beside some mighty mountains. Some call these the Rocky Mountains, which certainly makes sense when you see these peaks stretching to the sky. I've also heard the notion that these peaks create the Continental Divide. Seems to have something to do with the water flow from the mountains to the oceans. Maybe that is one of the things you youngsters could find out for me. The days are getting longer, but it's not much warmer. Don't know if it is because of the winds blowing off of the mountains or if it is just colder out West.

This morning, a stagecoach came thundering along the ridge trail with dust swirling, horses snorting, and bags and bundles up top bouncing. As the driver approached me, I heard a loud "Whoa!" and the stage came to a clambering stop. I was amazed at the skill that this driver had with that team of animals. If you looked closely, you could see six sets of reins wrapped securely around the driver's fingers, each being moved separately to get the horses to move to the right or the left or to stop. It was an amazing feat to see the control one person could have … especially one fairly small driver weighing about 130 pounds or so compared to the six horses that must have weighed more than 8,000 pounds all together.

I was glad to see him, and happier still when he said in a somewhat unusual sort of voice, "Howdy, you must be the Cowboy I've been hearing about along the trail."

I thought, "I'm not that unusual, for there must be hundreds of riders along this trail on any given week."

He continued, "Yep, I hear of this fine horse, a golden dog, and a gentleman cowboy riding on the Oregon Trail. I reckon that must be you."

"I suppose it is! What do they call you, sir?" I asked.

He replied, "Most call me Charley. Charley Parkhurst."

I acknowledged that I had heard of Charley as one of the bravest, wildest, most trustworthy stagecoach drivers in the West. He said "thanks" in that strange voice and said he needed to be going to make it to the next stop by nightfall. I said good-bye, wished him luck, and said I hoped we would meet again on the trail. He yelled back as he moved those horses to a steady trot, "Maybe we will. I'm through here again in a few weeks." I waved with my hat, and just as quickly as he arrived ... Charley was gone. The three of us just stood there by the trail looking toward a small dust cloud far in the distance.

The Cowboy (camped by a grove of trees with a small creek running through)

From *Galloping Along the Old West Trails*   © 1996   Teacher Ideas Press   1-800-237-6124.

Letter from the Stagecoach Driver

Whoa! This team is wild today. Because of five straight days of hard-hitting storms, we were stuck in a livery stable until the wind and snow let up. Six spirited geldings with extra energy is a challenge for even the best stagecoach driver.

I'm Charley, and I'm the driver of this stage. I work for the new Star Stagecoach Line and have been making this run for about seven months. It probably looks easy running a line of horses, but let me share a few things with you. It starts early in the morning when I lay out the harnesses, reins and bits, clips and clamps. I check every piece of leather for wear, and I check all parts of the coach for any signs of deterioration. If I find anything that could cause harm to my animals or passengers, I get it repaired before I do anything else. The horses were fed early, so they should be ready for their inspection. Each horse is groomed and checked for rocks or built-up material in their hooves. One rock would bruise the foot so badly that the whole team would have to be set aside for a day or two until the swelling let down. Either my assistant or I brush the horses, check eyes and ears, legs, and mouths, always looking for something that might place us in jeopardy. The company has extra horses, so discovering problems before we leave certainly has benefits. It takes two of us to lay the leather over each horse until finally all six horses are ready and in two lines. The reins are stretched to the driver's seat. We do one more check and, of course, make sure that the coach brake is tightly secured. The horses are ready. I grab the reins in two hands, wrapping each rein between a separate finger. These horses will respond to my touch as they have been trained. I've developed some powerful fingers. As we ride, my hands are continuing to adjust the reins to allow the horses just enough rein to pull, but not so much so they can run free. It's a balance, for sure. The dust can be incredible as 24 feet stir up the crusty soil and fling it in the air, creating a long cloud following the straight open trail. I sit on that wooden box bench and feel every bump and hole in the trail. I feel each mile as it disappears under the coach.

Stagecoach drivers are sure important for opening up the West. I'm responsible for the safety of my passengers, and when I have a mail shipment, I'm an agent of the U.S. government. Can't think of anyone more important as I carry supplies, mail, and new settlers west, and return with mail and word from those moved far away from friends and family. I've carried journalists, business people, "introduced" wives for marriage, generals, and outlaws. I once drove an English duke and his daughter who wanted to see the "Wild West." He arrived with his personal valet and a maid for the young woman. We stopped every night at the best hotel we could find, and he insisted on putting me up in the hotel as well. One day a right rear wagon wheel broke, and we had to spend the night out on the open range while I made repairs to the coach axle. The daughter and he got right in and helped cook the dinner and tend to the horses. I think he felt real proud of being a part of the new West.

I see things changing with each round trip. More people, new buildings, developing land, ranches and farms, and an excitement as I drive our new nation west. Hope to see you aboard. When in town, stop by the stage company office. If you hear someone yelling, "Ayyyyy," you'll know we're nearly ready to begin our journey.

Best to you on the trail,
Charley

Letter from the Stagecoach Driver

From *Galloping Along the Old West Trails* © 1996   Teacher Ideas Press   1-800-237-6124.

Activities

As the pioneers made their way West, towns and cities grew up along the trails. These were later connected by well-traveled roads. A popular but short-lived form of transportation was the bumpy, dusty, modest stagecoach.

Plotting the Stagecoach Line

Traveling by stagecoach offers many opportunities to sharpen students' math skills.

On a large map of the United States, plot the following trails:

* the Oregon Trail
* the Goodnight-Loving Trail
* the Shawnee Trail
* the Sedalia Trail
* the Western Trail

Using keys provided on the map, calculate the distance (in miles or kilometers) covered by each trail. Once the students have determined the distance of each trail, they can take charge of their own stagecoach line and plot out a route for their passengers. Determine cities for a starting point and final destination.

Students should think about how far the stagecoach could travel in one day. Consider that travel can only be done in daylight hours. Stops are required to rest and feed horses and passengers. Lodging for the night is also important. Of course, there are obstacles along the trail (a swollen river, a washed-out road, or bandits) and, depending on what time of the year it is, weather might interfere with the journey.

Advertise for New Customers

Have students design advertisements for the stagecoach line. Research a particular trail and include the information collected on the particular route (e.g., maybe it is the quickest, fastest, and safest passage to the West). Let the students use a variety of media and let their creativity soar even as they design their factual advertisements.

Stamp-eding Along the Trail

Postal stamps have long reflected artistically the epochs of American history. Recently, the U.S. Postal Service issued a collection of stamps depicting the Old West. The Legends of the West series includes such famous individuals as Buffalo Bill, Geronimo, Annie Oakley, Sacajawea, Bill Picket and many more. On the back of each stamp is a brief biographical sketch highlighting their achievements.

Students can design their own "postage stamps" based on the life or legend of an individual who made a difference in the expansion of the West. Have them include a brief biographical statement describing the accomplishments of the individual.

Before beginning the activity, ask your students to save the envelopes from mail received at their homes in a given week. Instruct them to cut out the upper right-hand corner (with the stamp) and bring the samples to class.

In cooperative groups, have students classify and compare the designs and features of the collected stamps. Call the local post office and ask if someone can come in and speak to the class (or perhaps plan a walking field trip to the local post office).

Now that the students have a working knowledge of stamps, have them each select a famous individual from the pioneer era and design a stamp. Instruct them to include a portrait of the subject within the design as well as background and icons that are representative of the chosen character's contributions to the Old West.

Creating Stamps

Objective

Students will design and create their own stamps.

Materials

★ 1 sheet of white drawing paper, cut 8 inches x 8 inches

★ Crayons

★ Felt-tip markers

★ Colored pencils

★ Paint

★ Scissors

Procedure

Now that the students have a working knowledge of stamps, have them select a famous individual from the pioneer era and design a stamp. Instruct them to include a portrait of the subject within the design as well as background and icons that are representative of the chosen character's contributions to the Old West. Emphasize that the illustration should include features that are big, bright, and bold. The design should cover the whole front of the paper. Lines in the drawing should be done in black or purple. Color should cover the majority of the design. Include in the lower right-hand corner the price for the postage.

One the stamp is finished, scallop cut the edge of all four sides and mount on a bulletin board for all to enjoy.

From *Galloping Along the Old West Trails* © 1996 Teacher Ideas Press 1-800-237-6124.

Letter 28
Life Doesn't Always
Smile on the Trip West

Today has been one of those days where sadness has touched us all. Life is not always sweet on the trail, and the stories don't always end with a happy tale or with the hero riding off into the sunset. Today, when passing through a town, I saw a family procession mourning the loss of a loved one. We moved off to the side of the street as a sign of respect, so they could pass unencumbered. I held Sierra against my leg so she wouldn't run off and disturb the family.

Death is a fact of the West. The undertaker, who is the first one to take care of the deceased, was standing in front of his office. Coincidentally, that's where I had also stopped to be out of the way. He told me that it is sad when someone close to us dies, but what is most sad is when that someone is a child. I agreed. Sometimes, the cause of death is an accident, a gunfight, or some unknown disease. Regardless, it is always a terrible loss. As the procession passed, I removed my hat and lowered my head. I wondered what it was like for this person in life. For just a moment it was very quiet, almost like time was standing still. All we could hear were the soft, muffled sobs coming from somewhere in the long line of mourners. I said a silent prayer, looked up to those majestic mountains, and thought about what the future had in store for me. Life will go on for the rest of us.

From *Galloping Along the Old West Trails*   © 1996 Teacher Ideas Press   1-800-237-6124.

I think I'll find a room, a hot meal, and settle in for the night. I'm going to look for a good livery stable for Kaper King (Sierra can stay there, too). I believe this might be a good night to be alone and think about what has happened to me and what might happen in the days ahead.

Good night.
The Cowboy

Letter from the Undertaker

Don't be afraid when you see me in town. I'm just doing my job, just like everyone else. I have a wife, two kids, a horse, and a small garden on the south side of my house.

I only wear a black suit when it's a funeral day. I'm the town's undertaker, and my name is Robert Thornhine. It is sad that people die, but one thing for sure, it will happen to everyone sooner or later. It's just a matter of time! When someone "passes on," the family needs to take care of the loved one and prepare him or her for a good burial. That's what I do. I provide respect and preparation to those who have "fallen."

People die from old age, accidents, and disease. The most tragic deaths are always those of the children. The West is full of tragedy and broken dreams. I try to give back something to the people who are on this earth, for however long that might be.

I either build a nice coffin myself or have it built by the town cabinetmaker. If it is a simple burial, which most are in our town, we use a plain box with cloth lining but no handles and no extra padding on the inside. I always try to find the individual's finest suit or dress for him or her to wear on the journey to the next world. The livery stable operator usually will loan me his wagon for the short trip to the town cemetery. We have no church here, so I may be called on to say a few words as comfort to any family and friends who might be attending. If it is a criminal, outlaw, or vagrant who has died, I still try to provide a respectful service, although it is sad that no one else is present at the burial.

I consider what I do part of the circle of life. People are born, and people will die. I do my part to help them when the final day has come. I hope I will have a chance to meet you all one day, preferably at a community event, like a barn raising or carnival, than a funeral. Take care.

Robert Thornhine

From *Galloping Along the Old West Trails* © 1996 Teacher Ideas Press 1-800-237-6124.

Activity

At most western burials, a minister, undertaker, or someone close to the deceased delivered a short eulogy praising the deceased.

Epitaphs and Eulogies

As a language arts activity, have your students write their own epitaph and eulogy. Have them look at their life's accomplishments and focus on the things that they want others to remember about them. This is a great tool for students to use in personal character analysis and an examination of their direction in life.

Extend the study by giving it a historical twist. Look at the burial rituals of Native Americans, or individuals who traveled west to pursue freedom of religious expression. Perhaps the students could research local history and contact the local historical society for information on cemeteries and information on prominent citizens whose final resting place is in the community.

Letter 29
Life and Legends

I'm in the area that they call the Nebraska Territories. I hear some call it Wyoming. Pretty country, but the terrain has changed. Today was a clear day with the breezes beckoning any man to keep moving west. Sometimes I think the wind is talking to me and helping me along the trail. Indians often talk about the spirits guiding them through life. I have heard stories about Indians who were guided by special spirits through snowstorms, blight, starvation, and war.

It appears that the Indians are losing their land and spirit as more and more settlers move through their precious wilderness. When I talked to that soldier back at the river, he told me that the Indians will be moved once more to large tracts of land called reservations, even though the government treaties said they would never be moved again. Although not spoken, we knew that the great Indian nations would not survive. Was this progress or the extermination of a proud people? I wondered what it would feel like if I were in that position.

I thought I had seen some Indians on the ridges as I passed through the narrow canyon gorges. I hoped they viewed me as only a visitor to the land and one who would cause no harm to those who call this their home. I would be honored to meet some of these people and learn more about them. Perhaps we could all learn something from people who respect and protect the earth.

As we rounded the corner on the narrow ledge of the trail, the ground beneath Kaper King's front legs gave way. We slipped down the hillside, Kaper King falling on his side and throwing me through the air, arms and legs flailing. All in slow motion, I saw Sierra scampering behind us as we slid and tumbled against the broken and sharp rocks. I could only see the blue of the sky, the white of the billowing clouds, and the gray brown of the rocky hillside. Then suddenly, all was dark.

I don't know exactly how long it had been, but I remember feeling first coldness and darkness and then warmth. Then darkness again. This occurred perhaps several times. I could hear voices and felt soft skin across my forehead. I thought maybe this was the sun from the day and the coldness of the night. I couldn't explain the voices.

As my eyes opened, I felt the soft breeze and gentle warm sun across my face. I looked up to see Kaper King standing by a small creek, his saddle, blanket, and bridle hanging on a short tree branch nearby. Sierra was curled up by my side. I was covered with a heavy blanket, and my head was resting on leaves beneath a woven pad. I sat up but could see no one. I felt a bandage tied across my temple and around my head. My boots were near my saddle. Someone had taken care of me after the fall and had stayed with me for I don't know how long, maybe days.

Sierra rustled to her feet and came to me, licking my face. I rubbed under her neck, and she quivered in delight. I got up slowly, put on my boots, washed my face, and was

---

Life and Legends

153

saddling up Kaper King when I looked to the mountain peak to the south and saw three figures on horseback watching me. I then knew that these were my protectors. Maybe they were spirits, but probably they were members of an Indian hunting party watching over me and offering me back my life. I gave a wave of my arms in acknowledgment. They waved back and turned their horses and disappeared over the ridge.

Just as I was about to mount Kaper King I looked to a large rock near where I had been resting and saw a picture scratched upon its vertical surface. It was a picture of many horses with wings flying down from a mountain pass. Could these have been the mythical "Sacred Dogs" I had heard about that protect the good people of the land? I hope to find out. I am just so thankful to be breathing the fresh morning air.

The Cowboy

Letter from a Native American

The Sun, the Moon, the Water, and the Earth guide my people. We are the proud ones. We have lived on this land in the plains and in the mountains for many moons. We share the beauty of the fawn, the strength of the bear, and the spirit of the long-winged bird as we make our way through the suns and moons of our lives. We are cleansed in the waterfalls and nourished by the heavens. We borrow from Nature's bounty, and we return to the earth our physical being.

Life has changed. No longer are my people free to share the land with the Buffalo or the Bear. No longer can we roam the mountains within the low clouds. No longer are my people free to be with the land. No longer are my people able to return their spirit to the earth.

The men with powerful tools have taken our lands. The soldiers have built giant houses to guard against my people. The eastern people form long wagon snakes, carving deep paths through the soil. Prairie fires burn our hearts, and the crackling smoke sticks kill Nature's gifts. The mighty iron horse continues to grow, bringing with it more fever, more heartache, more death. It is time for my people to find a new home as we did when we found this home.

From *Galloping Along the Old West Trails* © 1996 Teacher Ideas Press 1-800-237-6124.

What will become of our children, and their children, and their children?

We have been given the sacred dogs, yet that is not enough. We have been given the mighty wings of the eagle, yet that is not enough. We have been given the gift of the great spirit, yet that is not enough.

The newcomers do not understand our people, and they do not understand the gifts of the earth. It is our sorrow.

Winter Cloud

Activities

As we follow the movement west and the romanticism of the cowboy legend, we must not forget the Native Americans, whose civilization, land, and culture were decimated in the name of progress.

Coiled Pottery

The pottery of the Pueblo Indians was constructed using the "coiled" method. Have the students make clay pots using this procedure. Select a clay based on the type of equipment you have at school. If you have a kiln available, purchase the kind of clay that needs to be baked; if you do not have one, select a clay that will air dry.

Give each student a good-sized chunk of clay. Have the students roll long thin "snakes" out of the clay. These should be about one-half inch in diameter and about 1 foot long. Start coiling the clay to make a base, then work on building up the sides to create the shape of the pot. Use a damp sponge to smooth the sides and remove any lumps and bumps. Let air dry or bake in a kiln.

Stick Game

Some Native Americans would play this game using sticks and pebbles. Have the students recreate the game using tongue depressors.

Each student needs three game pieces. Have students draw or paint a snake on two of the pieces. On the third game piece, have the students draw or paint a stick figure of a person. The reverse side of all three game pieces should be left plain.

The game can also be played using pebbles or sticks. If collecting pebbles, look for those that are relatively flat on two sides. Sticks should be of equal length and sanded flat on two sides.

To play the game, each child takes turns tossing the game pieces. They hold all three game pieces between the hands and toss them all at once in the air. Each person's score is determined by how the pieces land. Total the point value based on the information below:

- ★ One plain, one snake, one person   3 points
- ★ All plain   4 points
- ★ Two snakes and one plain   5 points
- ★ Two plain and one snake   6 points
- ★ Any other combination   0 points

The student with the highest score wins the round.

From *Galloping Along the Old West Trails* © 1996 Teacher Ideas Press 1-800-237-6124.

Letter 30
Clank, Bang, and
Rattle

We're camped by a beautiful stream today waiting for a brief rain shower to pass. Sometimes these showers just come out of nowhere, suddenly appearing over the mountain. Today, it was the crackling of thunder and lightning as the white billowing cumulus clouds turned to gray and the sheets of electricity came bursting from the edges, much like a rabbit scampering in fright from a disturbance in the brush.

We found a nice rock overhang where Sierra and I could crawl into, and Kaper King was partially protected from the harshest elements. After about 30 minutes, the storm passed and it was clear again. To my amazement, to the west we could see a magnificent rainbow, like a fine woven quilt of brightly colored threads. That is the direction we are going, and I'm beginning to believe that a treasure awaits us at the end of that rainbow. Of course, it may not be gold or treasure to spend, but it certainly is a treasure being in the West with our journey's end but a few weeks away.

I mustn't become too confident, for men have perished in strange ways when they bristled with overconfidence. I heard that some drive wagons right off cliffs as they become intoxicated with the thought of the long struggle west being over. Another tale is told of a man who was yelling and laughing as the last range was in sight and

From *Galloping Along the Old West Trails* © 1996 Teacher Ideas Press 1-800-237-6124.

was then run over by his wagon and died less than five miles from the last crossing. So I shall hold my euphoria until the journey has come to an end. Several hundred miles remain for the three of us to endure.

Well, from right under that rainbow came a clanking and a banging from a wagon with wooden and canvas sides, jiggling and sliding down the wet trail. Sitting atop the driver's bench was a fellow whom I had not seen the likes of before. This "traveling salesman of the western territory" was driving a "shop on wheels." Certainly a handy and convenient way of buying goods if you should be in need. I best take stock of what I have and what I may need in the event his wares should be of interest. What would you buy if you were in the Oregon-Wyoming territory?

Your friends,
The Cowboy,
Kaper King, and
Sierra

Clank, Bang, and Rattle

Letter from the
Traveling Salesman

The folks in the string of towns along the trails call me "Drummer" Benson. The term drummer refers to a traveling salesman or peddler. It's a good job, and I really love it. Not for a married man but for me, being single and full of adventure yet wanting to do well in business, it is the perfect mix. I am fortunate that I am able to see and enjoy this beautiful country as well as to meet mostly real nice people. I'm sure I'm contributing to the growing West. The traveling salesman provides an important service to folks heading west or settling on the frontier. I'm real proud of the service I provide. Let's get one thing settled right off. I am not the dishonest "snake oil," shifty salesman who sometimes moves around these parts with the carnival. I have accompanied the carnival from time to time, but my products are fine, and I will stand behind them. If you are not satisfied, I'll return your money.

I have sold products for just one company, such as the time I worked for a pharmacist selling various drugs and medicinal products to stores and doctors. But now I'm kind of a general store on wheels, traveling around to folks in the outlying areas, away from the main cities and towns, and trying to provide them with the things they need. My wagon is stocked with books, sewing needles, saws and plows, clothes, pots and pans, and even music boxes for special occasions. I have some very special lace that I bought from another salesman coming from Europe.

I charge a bit more than the store owners in town for some items and less for others. It depends on what my expenses are, how far I have to travel, and what the market will bear. I always try to be fair so that customers will be happy and purchase from me the next time I come through.

Most of the folks are glad to see me when I come around. I bring them products, but I also bring them news and stories of what is happening in the territories, as well as back home in the East. I'm often invited into the homes of my regular customers. In the summer, we sit on the small front porches and tell stories and share the news. It's kind of like having a growing family all over the country.

I prefer cash for the goods I sell, but sometimes my buyers want to trade instead. I'll take homemade preserves, quilts, or products that are sewn or made at home. I also take furs in trade for some of my products. Of course, I can only accept these items if I'm sure I can get a better price later and make a profit.

People often ask me about my future. I tell them that I like the traveling, but someday I probably will meet the right woman and settle down in one place and raise a family. Then, I'll be on the other side of the wagon, buying some of my necessary items from the next generation of "drummers." Oh, by the way, I have some great hard candy here if you are interested.

Hope to see you in the next town,
Mr. Theodore Benson

P.S. Have you seen a fellow by the name of Strauss? Mr. Levi Strauss? He had some canvas for sale. I told him I would be happy to take it back to St. Louis and sell it there. He said he might first try to sell it in a mining camp. I hope he did all right. Sure hate to think of him getting stuck with all that cloth. If you see him, remind him of my offer.

Letter from the Traveling Salesman   161

Activities

Traveling salesmen—drummers or peddlers as they were called—followed and cultivated customers in the West. They provided goods and services that were not readily available in outlying areas. On their cart they carried a vast array of items, from pots and pans, to medicines and elixirs, to books and stationery, as well as clothing.

Sell Your Wares

Your students can become the drummers of today. Tell them that they are to imagine a place where people are beginning to settle. The new community has shelter, food, water, electricity, and phone lines, but little else. Instruct them to make an inventory of things they could take to sell to this community. Let them consider what the most desirable items would be. What would they consider to be a fair markup for profit?

The Most for Your Money

Have the students create a list of items that they think might be purchased from traveling drummers of the western era. Assign prices to these items. Ask the children to write mathematical word problems based on money and purchases. Create the next math test using their problems. Here are two examples.

Mr. Farley needed a bottle of "Magic Elixir" (75 cents) to soothe his cough, a copper skillet (55 cents) because the old one broke a handle, and seven blue buttons (3 cents each) for a dress his wife was making. How much money did he spend that day?

Mrs. Templeton wanted a box of stationery for writing correspondence. The salesperson had many boxes from which to choose. One box contained 50 sheets of pearl-colored paper for 67 cents. Another box had 75 sheets of white stationery for 45 cents. The nicest stationery was white with lace cutouts, but cost 35 cents for 10 sheets. Which box was the best buy for the money?

A Stetson and the Falling Cards

Here's a cowboy magic trick. Lay a cowboy hat on the floor with the opening facing the ceiling. Ask a bystander to hold the cards about four feet above the mouth of the hat and drop them into the hat, one at a time. The person will most likely miss each time. You then have your turn and never miss a shot. The trick is to be sure and hold the card parallel to the floor and then release it.

The Silver Dollar and the Bandanna

The trail drive was long and hard. In the evenings the weary cowpokes entertained themselves with card games, storytelling—and maybe a little magic. Impress your class with this magic trick.

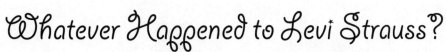

   For this activity use a half dollar as you don't see too many silver dollars in circulation.

   Place the bandanna on a flat surface and lay the coin in the middle. Take hold of the opposite corners and tightly grasp the fabric between your forefingers and thumbs. Stretch the bandanna taut and the coin will balance in the gutter formed on the edge of the bandanna. The audience will not see that the coin is resting in a gutter; instead it will appear to be balancing on the edge of the bandanna.

Whatever Happened to Levi Strauss?

Have students find out what Levi Strauss did to get rid of all the extra canvas he had.

From *Galloping Along the Old West Trails*   © 1996   Teacher Ideas Press   1-800-237-6124.

Letter 31
By Ourselves in the Woods

It is a sunny afternoon riding west, near a place called Farewell Bend, which is a ways outside of Fort Boise. A sudden chill hangs in the air as the wind whistles through the lonesome pines scattered along the hillside. The smell of fresh vegetation and wet earth fills my lungs, and each step we take brings us closer to our dreams. The days are getting longer as winter fades. We can travel greater distances because light is the key to moving with safety. Of course, we could never move forward hour after hour without many rest stops. For the three of us, it is essential that we stop every couple of hours and rest, drink some water, and take time for Kaper King to graze and Sierra to take a quick nap.

Up ahead, I can see a figure approaching. Haven't seen or talked to anyone (except Kaper King and Sierra and an occasional squirrel) for a couple of days. A very tall, slim man wearing a buckskin vest came across our encampment. He introduced himself as a trapper. I invited him to sit, and the two of us shared some of the dried meat he pulled from his satchel and some bread that I had been carrying for a few days. We talked, we ate (the bread was a bit stale and dry but tasted OK because we were hungry), and we shared our plans for the future. He had seen lots of men and families moving west. He found a good life trapping and trading animal pelts in the northern territories. Game was plentiful, and trading had been good. After several hours, I decided to stay where I was for the night; my newest friend decided to go farther east to

---

By Ourselves in the Woods

From *Galloping Along the Old West Trails* © 1996 Teacher Ideas Press 1-800-237-6124.

meet buyers at Three Island crossing and then finally to Fort Hall.

As we bid good-bye, he reached up on his horse and pulled a large piece of cloth from his mound of pelts. The cloth turned out to be a blanket. The trapper said he had received this special blanket from a small Indian tribe some months past, and he wanted me to have it for the remainder of my journey. It was large enough to wrap around me on chilly days while riding, or for sleeping comfortably at night. It was a light color with bands of brown and black made from the natural dyes of plants and berries. I appreciated both the gesture of this trapper and the spirit it held from the natives of this land. It was indeed a true treasure. We shook hands, and he disappeared into the forest.

I used that blanket that night as I listened to a strange sound in the darkness. It was a "Whoooo, whoooo" sound. I looked up to the tree limbs and could see the full-rounded shapes of some kind of bird sitting majestically watching over me. Truly, those birds made beautiful music that gently put me to sleep.

The Cowboy

By Ourselves in the Woods 165

From *Galloping Along the Old West Trails* © 1996 Teacher Ideas Press 1-800-237-6124.

Letter from the Fur Trapper

My pack horse is weighed down with pelts after a good month of trapping in the snowy mountains. It's been extra cold this year, but I believe that winter has finally broken. Seems like we had to wait out longer storms before heading back down to the base camp, where my small cabin is located. When you're on the mountain, just you and your horse, you begin to think. You think about trapping, you think about the Indians, you think about people back in St. Louis. I've been out here for many years now, and I know these mountains like the top of my right foot. Oh, forgot to tell you, my name is Jonathan Shorr.

Trappers like me have aided the settlers going west. We have traveled these trails and can lead folks through them with ease. I've spent time with explorers who work for the railroad, and we share our discoveries of trails running through the mountains. I spent almost a year as a guide for the government when they were looking for a location to build a new military outpost. I'm not sure we really need more government soldiers out here. It's causing a lot of problems with the Indians, who believe this to be their land. They were here first, so I think I agree. I get along well with the local Indian tribes. They know me and welcome me into their camps. We trade at least twice a year. They provide me with pelts, and I have store-bought things that they desire. It works out well, and everyone is satisfied. I sense, however, that this is going to change as more and more settlers come through here.

Well, anyway, trapping is a good but hard life. I'm outdoors in the quiet wilderness and I make a good amount of money. St. Louis and the eastern states are the greatest sources of customers for my furs. I understand that the Europeans are also very anxious to receive the furs of beavers and other animals to make hats and clothing.

From *Galloping Along the Old West Trails* © 1996 Teacher Ideas Press 1-800-237-6124.

Someday you might follow me when I'm on the line trapping. I'm pretty fierce to look at with my long hair and beard. My clothes are made from the furs I trap, so some call me "Mountain Man," and others confuse me with the Indians of the area. I usually carry on my person a long sharp knife, a small hatchet, and a rifle. When I catch an animal, I usually skin the pelt immediately. If the weather allows, I stretch it until it is dried in the sun. I use what meat I can, dry some for the coming weeks, and leave the remainder for hungry animals. I travel softly on foot, with my packhorse two steps behind, always watching, always listening, always learning. I'm not sure if you would want to be a trapper, but for me and the West, it has been good.

Jonathan Shorr

Activity

In the search for pelts, a trapper would study the ground for evidence of an animal's presence. A keen eye would not only uncover the tracks of the specific prey but would also discover traces of other wild varmints that roamed beyond man's reach.

Paw Prints

Have your students create paw prints using the templates in figure 31.1. Trace the paw prints onto thick tagboard, then cut out the pieces.

Create tracks using plaster of paris. Mix the plaster to a medium-thick consistency. Too thick, and you will never see your thumb again. Pour the mixture into an aluminum pie tin or Styrofoam plate. Carefully press each tagboard piece into the plaster, making sure to maintain the integrity of the paw print's shape. Add pressure to form an imprint in the mixture. Let stand overnight to dry. When dry, paint the plaster with brown tempera paint. To add a realistic look, apply a thin coat of glue to the mold and sprinkle dirt and dried grass over it.

From *Galloping Along the Old West Trails* © 1996 Teacher Ideas Press   1-800-237-6124.

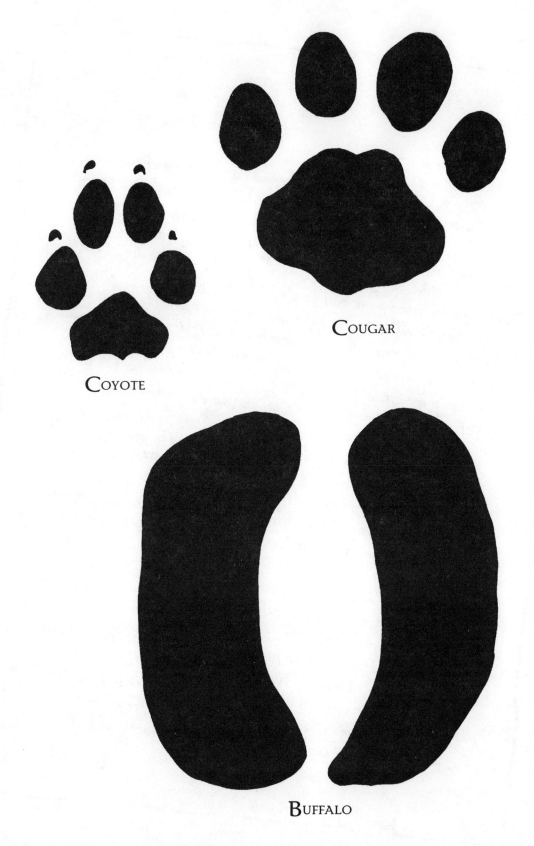

COUGAR

COYOTE

BUFFALO

FIGURE 31.1 PAW AND HOOF PRINTS

Activity   169

Letter 32
Who Finds Our Way

Before the tall trapper departed our small camp, he told me of a couple—husband and wife—who were explorers in this territory. I sure would like to meet up with them. I would imagine they have a lot of great stories to tell. Being an explorer is like being an inventor. You really are the first! I realized that someone had to chart this wilderness for the first time. Often it is the explorers who take on this perilous job. Sometimes they are just hunters or settlers who send one of the crew miles out ahead to find the best route around or through a mountain pass. Explorers are the ones who tell us it is safe to cross the river here, or maybe we should cross it five miles downstream.

I knew that some of the eastern railroad companies hired explorers to chart the best place to lay track. After all, you can't just put down the rails as you go. What would happen if you did it that way? Other explorers, I hear, work as trappers, and some sign on as guides for the wagon trains. Others work for the government or the U.S. Army. Imagine if we had no trails and just headed off following the sun. Shoot, maybe we'd get there and maybe we wouldn't. The explorers have a rough life, but it must be exciting.

Sometimes, as I lay on my back, when the last embers of the campfire are quietly flickering out, I stare up at the stars and think about what is out there. Maybe someday man will explore the heavens as well. I suppose that's crazy talk. There's nothing out in the night but darkness and small lights. So I

Who Finds Our Way

From *Galloping Along the Old West Trails* © 1996 Teacher Ideas Press 1-800-237-6124.

should say that the explorers are really the silent heroes of the West.

Darn, where is that Sierra? She ran off again chasing some little varmint. Never know who is really chasing who, as Sierra isn't the bravest of dogs. But she sure is lovable. I hear her now barking and howling. Must have some little critter up a tree. She never catches anything, but she sure does have a good time! Let me know if you hear anything from the explorers.

Probably in the next week or so we will meet up with the grand Columbia River. I feel something exciting beginning to happen around us. A few more settlers can be seen on the trail, and out in the distance we can see a cabin or two where folks have settled a homestead.

Warmest wishes,
The Cowboy, Kaper King,
and Sierra

Who Finds Our Way

From *Galloping Along the Old West Trails* © 1996 Teacher Ideas Press 1-800-237-6124.

Letter from the
Explorer

I'm opening up the West! My name is Alfred Hansbaugh, and I'm an explorer for the railroad. My job is to explore areas that may be suitable for the railroad and do a preliminary chart so that the planners, geographers, and geologists will have an idea of what they are getting into when they are summoned to the area.

For five years I worked with a man by the name of James Yarnell. James and I covered a lot of territory and got into some mighty difficult scrapes. Now, I am working with the best of the best, my wife, Rose Hansbaugh. It isn't uncommon for a husband and wife to be hired on as explorers. The long days and need for teamwork make this a suitable alliance for couples who get along well.

I remember the first time I headed out west from the Mississippi. Those first 40 miles seemed like forever. Every turn, every hill, every gorge was new and needed charting. Now, from existing explorations, we search for new routes west for the railroad. There is so much to consider. We have to look beyond what our eyes can see. If we take the train one route and then find an impassable mountain, our time and the time of the architects are wasted, not to mention the cost of it all. We must be very careful to see if the slope is too steep or what will happen to the mountain in the winter. Would the track be subject to fewer snowdrifts if we laid the track on the other side of the mountain, away from the

From *Galloping Along the Old West Trails* © 1996 Teacher Ideas Press 1-800-237-6124.

winter winds? What about avalanches? Will falling trees pose a threat? Can we more easily build bridges over rivers here or upstream? Will the engines have the power to make it up the steep inclines? Can we find fuel to maintain the fire in the engines over long distances?

Most of what Rose and I do is routine: riding, walking, and writing in our books. Rose also does the drawings so that the planners in St. Louis will know what we are describing. We have spent six months at a time out in the wild. We know how to hunt, build shelters, and make friends with the people of this land. We've been shot at, held down by storms, washed down streams in floods, and chased by hungry bears. An explorer has to be able to survive on the land. When you can't hear and sense the unexpected, when you look and go southwest when you should have gone northwest, it's time to think about settling down and passing the hat to someone else.

Rose and I love the frontier. We consider ourselves the inventors of the West, for most of what we see and draw has never been seen by the white man before. A little piece of the West will always be ours, as we saw its adventure and beauty first. You and I will probably never meet, because Rose and I will almost always be somewhere off the regular trails and paths. But you just look up to the mountains or across the plains and know that we are out there.

Alfred Hansbaugh

Letter from the Explorer   173

Activities

When early explorers ventured deep into the wilderness, they had little idea of what lay before them, yet they forged on charting and mapping the country. Some of these early pioneers are well remembered by the rivers, mountains, and passes that bear their names. Others, whose names were only known by the wind, are long forgotten. These brave men and women truly made the reality of westward expansion possible.

Map Reading

Today's urban and rural explorers would be lost without their maps. Instruct your students on the process of map reading. Study longitude and latitude, cardinal and intermediate directions, and how to read a key on a flat map. Identify political and natural boundaries. Collect maps of your city or state and ask the students to locate specific cities and towns. (Travel clubs can be a good source for free maps.) Have the students determine the best route between specified points and calculate the distance using the information provided on the maps.

Salt and Flour Relief Maps

Objective

Students will create salt and flour relief maps that show the regions of a given area.

Materials

* ★ 2 cups flour
* ★ 1 cup salt
* ★ $\frac{1}{2}$ cup water
* ★ maps
* ★ tempera paint

Procedure

Instruct the students to mix the flour and salt together, then slowly add water. (You may need more, you may need less.) Mix to a consistency that will hold a shape.

On a piece of cardboard, have the students draw the outline of the map. They can spread a thin layer of dough over the entire area, then *slowly* begin to add dough to the areas that represent the higher elevations. Let the map dry one or two days. Using tempera paint, students can highlight the regional areas (e.g., coastal areas, blue; valleys, green; deserts, yellow; and mountains, brown).

Topographical Maps

The topographical map is a wonderful tool for helping young explorers see what lies ahead. Figure 32.1 illustrates such a map. The circles on the map represent a mountain or protrusion in the earth's surface. The smaller the circle, the nearer the peak. The distance between each line represents the same change in altitude, for example, 100 feet. The lines that are closer together indicate that the terrain is steeper than the area represented by the lines that are farther apart. Thus, a hiker reading a "topo" map would probably be cautious of areas featuring many tight lines, as these would indicate a cliff or a very treacherous, steep climb. Explore the features of a topographical map with your students. Problem solve such dilemmas as, Which way would you go to reach the top?

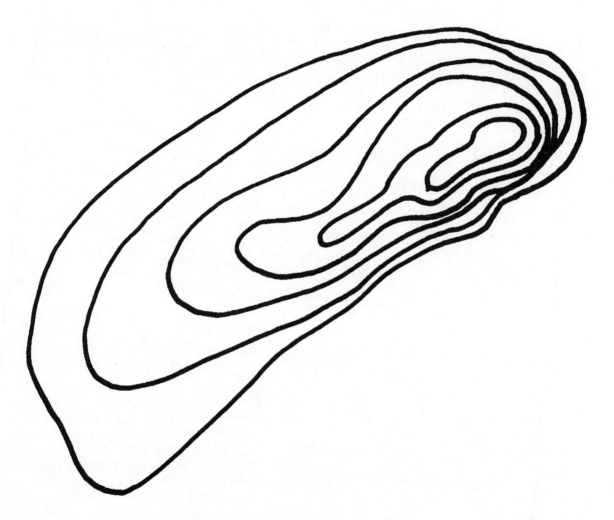

FIGURE 32.1 A TOPOGRAPHICAL MAP (FROM LINE TO LINE EQUALS 100 FEET IN ALTITUDE)

Activities   175

Letter 33
Soon a New Beginning

We've been following fairly close to the Columbia River for the last week, having left Fort Dalles as the last major center, where we saw lots of activity. The fort and outbuildings sit above the river gorge, looking down on the territory for miles of uninterrupted vistas. That was six days ago. Two days before that, it rained harder than I could have ever imagined. Had to get in from all that water. We found a small inn near the fort, which was warm when we entered, with a glowing and crackling fire in a large stone fireplace. I left Kaper King under a coverlike awning by the side of the building. He stayed quite dry, although the cold may not have been to his liking. His winter coat is still quite fluffy, adding extra protection from the elements. When the real spring thaw comes, that soft horsehair will begin to shed like falling snowflakes from a white cloud. Sounds pretty, doesn't it? But getting horsehair in your blanket and britches and down your shirt can really make you itch. Losing and growing hair on our animals is Nature's way of taking care of all creatures as we adapt to the environment. My, how much wisdom I have gained during my travels!

Well, back to the fire. Must have taken months to build such an elegant fireplace. Natural rocks piled one on top of another held together by molded mortar, with a beautiful carved wooden mantle across the top. Two carved wooden hawks adorned the sides as though they were watching each person who stood before that powerful blaze. I sat down at a small table and ordered a bowl of stew. The innkeeper soon returned with a large metal bowl filled high with potatoes, chunks of meat, and other vegetables in a rich, aromatic dark gravy. A plate of golden brown dark bread

Soon a New Beginning

From *Galloping Along the Old West Trails* © 1996 Teacher Ideas Press 1-800-237-6124.

roughly cut with visible seeds of grain was the perfect accompaniment to this traveler's feast. You all may not think much of this meal from where you are, but, to me, it is like food for royalty. It warmed me up from the tips of my toes to the top of my head.

The rain kept falling. It rained so hard during the night that every traveler within 20 miles seemed to end up in that little inn. We all talked and shared stories. Some were happy and others were sad, all a part of the journey west. Every now and then, I would get up and go out and check on Kaper King. You could hardly see three feet in front of you for the wall of water dropping from the sky and pouring off the steep roof.

You may wonder where Sierra was during all this. Keeping her buddy Kaper King company? Watching out for our possessions? Protecting me at my feet? No, she was curled up on the hearth by that warm, blazing fire. By morning, the storm had passed, and all of the travelers slowly emptied into the muddy street to resume the trek west.

The next several days the sky stayed clear, the air was fresh. Each morning we had the rising sun to our backs until evening began to fall and the sun was ahead once again, slowly signaling the end of another day. Following the river off to our right shoulder offered special security as we knew it would lead us to a worthwhile destination. That, of course, is if we follow it downhill. Also, it is good to know that there will always be a plentiful source of water for the animals and me.

It seemed to smell different as we continued our move west. The trees were taller, the ground was moist and dark, and sometimes I thought we were getting so close to the end of the journey that we could smell the salt air of the great

---

Soon a New Beginning   177

Pacific. As we came over the rise in the hill, before us was a green, tree-covered valley where two mighty rivers came together like two giant silver ribbons.

We continued slowly with each step, as this was the day we had lived for for so long. Mixed with the joy of this moment was a sadness to know that it was near an end. I thought clearly about the many months which had passed, the wonderful people we had met, how much we had learned, and all the adventure, some happy and some sad. We were the fortunate ones. We could now look ahead and know that our future would be filled with new adventure and unknown events. Sure, we were just a traveling man, a fine horse, and a golden dog, but the three of us were looking out over the edge of this great continent. Together we had made it.

I slid down off Kaper King, and with Sierra at my leg, the three of us stood silently looking off to the west, to the end of the Oregon Trail. Ten, maybe fifteen more miles, and we would come to the ferryboat crossing between the Columbia and the Willamette rivers. When our feet clamber aboard that wooden river ferryboat, our miracle will have come true. The journey west will have officially ended, but it will then be the time for us to decide whether we will make our home in the Oregon Territory or whether we will take the Applegate Trail south to the Lassen Trail into the great state of California. I've always dreamed of California.

Your friends,
The Cowboy, Sierra,
and Kaper King

Soon a New Beginning

Bibliography

Student Book List

Storybooks

White Dynamite and Curly Kidd by Bill Martin and
    John Archambault
Rosie and the Rustlers by Roy Gerrard
Armadillo Rodeo by Jan Brett
Cowboys by Glen Rounds
The Cowboy and the Black-Eyed Pea by Tony Johnston
Where the Buffalo Roam by Jacqueline Geis
Nature's Footprints in the Desert by Q. L. Pearce and W. J. Pearce
Who Lives on the Prairie? by Ron Hirschi
Little House on the Prairie by Laura Ingalls Wilder

Reference Books

Cowboys by Rick Steber
Cowboys of the Wild West by Russell Freedman
Cowboys: A Library of Congress Book by Martin W. Sandler
EyeWitness Books: Cowboy
Reflections of a Black Cowboy by Robert Miller
My First Book of Cowboy Songs by Dolly M. Moon

Coloring Books/Reference Books

Cowgirls by Bellerophon Books
Cowboys by Bellerophon Books
The Black Cowboy by Bellerophon Books
Cowboys of the Old West by David Rickman
An Educational Coloring Book of Cowboys by Spizzirri Publishing

Horses

EyeWitness Books: Horse
Album of Horses by Marguerite Henry
Draw 50 Horses by Lee J. Ames

For More Information

Barry, J. *Bloody Kansas*. New York: Franklin Watts, 1972.

Barry, L. *The Beginning of the West 1540–1854*. Topeka, KS: Kansas State Historical Society, 1972.

Coit, Margaret L. *The Sweep Westward*. California State Department of Education, 1967.

Cole, D. *Atlas of American History*. Boston: Ginn & Company, 1967.

Edroes, Richard. *Saloons of the Old West*. New York: Alfred A. Knopf, 1979.

Faber, Doris, and Faber, Harold. *American Government: Great Lives*. New York: Charles Scribner's Sons, 1988.

Frandin, D. *Kansas in Word and Picture*. Canada: Regensteiner Pub. Enterprise, 1980.

Freedman, Russel. *Cowboys of the Wild West*. New York: Clarion Books, 1985.

Gunby, L. *Early Farm Life*. Toronto: Crabtree Publishing Company, 1983.

Hanauer, Elsie V. *No Foot, No Horse*. Fort Collins, CO: Caballus, 1974.

Hawkins, Nancy, and Hawkins, Arthur. *The American Regional Cookbook*. Englewood Cliffs, NJ: Prentice-Hall, 1976.

Hine, Robert V. *The American West*. Boston: Little, Brown, 1984.

Hunt, Gaillard. *Life in America One Hundred Years Ago*. New York: Harper and Brothers, 1914.

Johnston, Tony, and Ludwig, Warren. *The Cowboy and the Black-Eyed Pea*. New York: G. P. Putnam's Sons, 1992.

Keegan, M. *Oklahoma*. New York: Abbeville Press, 1975.

Krause, B. *Collecting Paper Money for Pleasure and Profit: A Comprehensive Guide for Collectors and Investors*. Ohio: Betterway Books, 1992.

Martin, C. *Whiskey and Wild Women*. New York: Hart, 1974.

Moon, Dolly M. *My First Book of Cowboy Songs*. New York: Dover, 1982.

Murdoch, David. *EyeWitness Books: Cowboy*. New York: Alfred A. Knopf, 1993.

Ray, Delia. *A Nation Torn*. New York: Lodestar Books, 1990.

Rich, E. *The Heritage of Kansas*. Lawrence, KS: University of Kansas Press, 1960.

Russell, S. *The Farm*. New York: Parent's Magazine Press, 1970.

Shaw, J. *The American Girl Collection: Kristen*. Madison, WI: Pleasant, 1986.

Steber, Rick. *Cowboys*. Prineville, OR: Bonanza, 1988.

Street, F. *The Kaw: The Heart of a Nation*. New York: Rinehart and Company, 1941.

Wells, R. *Waiting for the Evening Star*. New York: Dial Books for Young Readers, 1993.

About the Authors

Gary M. Garfield is a professor of education at California State Polytechnic University, Pomona. For 20 years his primary focus has been the preparation of new teachers. Recent efforts have been directed in the area of integrated social studies

curriculum with telecommunications for preservice and in-service classroom teachers. His areas of university teaching include reading instruction, educational psychology, dynamics of teaching in a pluralistic society, general methodology, organization of schooling, clinical supervision, early field experience, and introduction to classrooms and schools. Garfield has presented at national, state, regional, and local professional conferences and workshops. He is an educational consultant for school districts within a variety of teaching areas. Garfield holds California teaching credentials in elementary and secondary education, special education, administrative services, and community college. He has an earned doctorate in educational management.

Suzanne McDonough is currently a technology mentor teacher and fourth-grade classroom teacher in the Mountain View School District, Ontario, California. A teacher of both primary and upper-grade students, with an emphasis on thematic approach to elementary school teaching using telecommunications in the classroom. McDonough has been a presenter at national, state, and regional association conferences and county offices of education. She serves as an educational consultant committed to equal access to information for all learners.